FREE SPEECH AND POLITICAL PROTEST

PROBLEMS IN POLITICAL SCIENCE
under the editorial direction of NEAL RIEMER, *University of Wisconsin-Milwaukee*

WESTERN EUROPE: WHAT PATH TO INTEGRATION? *edited by* CAROL EDLER BAUMANN, *University of Wisconsin-Milwaukee*

THE REPRESENTATIVE: TRUSTEE? DELEGATE? PARTISAN? POLITICO? *edited by* NEAL RIEMER, *University of Wisconsin-Milwaukee*

FREE SPEECH AND POLITICAL PROTEST *edited by* MARVIN SUMMERS, *University of Wisconsin-Milwaukee*

OTHER VOLUMES IN PREPARATION

PROBLEMS IN POLITICAL SCIENCE

Free Speech and Political Protest

EDITED WITH AN INTRODUCTION BY
Marvin Summers
University of Wisconsin-Milwaukee

D. C. HEATH AND COMPANY BOSTON

Table of Contents

v

The Clash of Ideas

FREEDOM OF EXPRESSION

Whoever would overthrow the Liberty of the Nation, must begin by subduing the Freedom of Speech. . . .
Without Freedom of Thought, there can be no such Thing as Wisdom; and no such Thing as publick Liberty, without Freedom of Speech. . . .

CATO'S LETTERS, 1720

But when men have realized that time has upset many fighting faiths, they may come to believe even more than they believe the very foundations of their own conduct that the ultimate good desired is better reached by free trade in ideas—that the best test of truth is the power of the thought to get itself accepted in the competition of the market, and that truth is the only ground upon which their wishes safely can be carried out.

MR. JUSTICE HOLMES DISSENTING IN
Abrams v. United States, 1919

BAD TENDENCY

[T]o punish (as the law does at present) any dangerous or offensive writing, which when published, shall on a fair and impartial trial be adjudged of a *pernicious tendency,* is necessary for the preservation of peace and good order, of government, and religion, the only solid foundations of civil liberty.

BLACKSTONE'S COMMENTARIES, 1769

CLEAR-AND-PRESENT-DANGER DOCTRINE

The question in every case is whether the words used are used in such circumstances that they will bring about the substantive evils that Congress has a right to prevent.

MR. JUSTICE HOLMES IN
SCHENCK V. UNITED STATES, 1919

PREFERRED POSITION

The case confronts us again with the duty our system places on this Court to say where the individual's freedom ends and the state's power begins. Choice on that border, now as always delicate, is perhaps more so where the usual presumption supporting legislation is balanced by the preferred place given in our scheme to the great, the indispensable democratic freedoms secured by the First Amendment.

MR. JUSTICE RUTLEDGE IN
Thomas v. Collins, 1944

GRAVITY-OF-THE-EVIL TEST

Overthrow of the Government by force and violence is certainly a substantial enough interest for the Government to limit speech.

MR. JUSTICE VINSON IN
Dennis v. United States, 1951

In each case [courts] must ask whether the gravity of the 'evil' discounted by its improbability, justifies such invasion of free speech as is necessary to avoid the danger.

JUDGE LEARNED HAND IN
United States v. Dennis, 1950

CONSTITUTIONAL ABSOLUTES

It is my belief that there are "absolutes" in our Bill of Rights, and that they were put there on purpose by men who knew what words meant, and meant their prohibitions to be "absolutes."

JUSTICE HUGO L. BLACK, "THE BILL OF RIGHTS,"
New York University Law Review, 1960

The First Amendment seems to me to be a very uncompromising statement. It admits of no exceptions. It tells us that the Congress . . . [is] . . . denied any authority whatever to limit the political freedom of the citizens of the United States.

ALEXANDER MEIKLEJOHN
Political Freedom, 1960

Introduction

On March 2, 1961, a group of Negro students converged on the state capitol of South Carolina carrying placards and singing freedom songs. The declared purpose of their protest was to express dissatisfaction with "discriminatory actions against Negroes" and to demand that "laws which prohibit Negro privileges" be repealed. This demonstration had lasted for about forty-five minutes, attracting a crowd of 200 to 300 curious onlookers, when the police intervened and told the students that they must disperse within fifteen minutes or they would be arrested. When the demonstration continued, 187 students were taken into custody and charged with breach of the peace.

This incident contains the classic elements in the conflict between freedom of expression and the need for public order. The students had a grievance and felt they had a constitutional right to express their dissatisfaction. Indeed, free speech, freedom of the press, the right to assemble and to petition for redress of grievances are specifically recognized by the First Amendment to the U.S. Constitution. The quality of our democracy depends in large measure on a wide-ranging freedom to communicate ideas, to form political associations, to take political action and to express opposition to government policies.

Yet every government has an obligation to maintain public order for the welfare of persons within its jurisdiction and to protect other legitimate social interests. In fact, the right to expression and political protest can be sustained only within the context of social order. Excessive concern about public order and stability may create oppressive conditions, yet unrestrained expression and political activity can cause serious social disorder. Normally, the conflict between freedom of expression and the need for public order ranges safely within these two extremes; however, government must be prepared to manage the tension created by these potentially opposing interests.

The constitutional guidelines around which we try to resolve these tensions are anchored in the First Amendment:

1

Congress shall make no law respecting an establishment of religion, or prohibiting the free exercise thereof; or abridging the freedom of speech, or of the press; or the right of the people peaceably to assemble, and to petition the government for a redress of grievances.

In our system of government, the Supreme Court plays an important role in interpreting the First Amendment and determining the boundaries of expression and protest. In *Edwards v. South Carolina* (1963), the case arising from the demonstration described above, the Court upheld the claim of the Negro students and reversed their conviction for breach of the peace. The constitutional doctrine for making that determination is, however, unsettled. During the 1940's, the Court gave a broad interpretation to freedom of expression; in the 1950's, the scope of First Amendment guarantees seemed to have been narrowed. The 1960's pose new problems which strain existing doctrine and point to the need for reinterpreting the ancient rights of the First Amendment.

The purpose of this volume is to invite participation in that continuing reinterpretation. Part I provides an historical orientation to the problem. The first selection describes the emergence of the idea of free expression in England, and the second reports our early American experiences. In both instances, the authors point to freedom of the press as the source of important precedents and legal doctrines relevant to a general discussion of freedom of expression. Part II focuses on the efforts of the Supreme Court to develop constitutional doctrine for determining the permissible limits to expression and political protest. Part III deals with three contemporary problems which raise difficult First Amendment issues, namely, libel actions against newspapers by government officials, student protest against the Selective Service system, and demonstrations for Negro rights.

Historical Background

Leonard W. Levy, in "A Tradition of Suppression," briefly recounts the emergence in England of the right to express political dissent, and its survival over the challenge of the King's censor, the concepts of criminal and seditious libel, the Star Chamber, and the cruelty of the common law. From the earliest days of printing, English sovereigns had exercised the prerogative of licensing all printed matter. It was against this type of prior censorship that John Milton inveighed in his famous essay, *Areopagitica.* Although the general practice of licensing went out of existence in 1694, it did not usher in freedom of the press. Writers and publishers still faced the threat of libel prosecutions. Generally, libel laws provide for punishment, after the fact of publication, for any injury caused by the printed word. Contrary to Sir William Blackstone, who defined freedom of the press as merely the absence of prior censorship, the severe penalties meted out for an assortment of libels proved every bit as oppressive as the King's censor.

Of the various forms of libel, seditious libel is the most ominous threat to political dissent. It is vaguely defined as any expression which defames, brings into ill repute, or lessens respect for the government, its officers, and its symbols of authority. In times of national crisis, it is tempting for an harrassed and insecure ruling party to equate legitimate criticism with seditious libel. Despite waves of suppression, threats, and severe punishment, some Englishmen did criticize the government and nurtured the idea that freedom of political dissent was an important civil liberty.

Both the common law with its libel precedents and the tradition of free political criticism were transplanted to the American colonies, and the continued tension between these legacies of our English heritage is reflected throughout our early history. The trial of Peter Zenger in 1735 and the adoption of the First Amendment to the Constitution in 1791 stand as landmarks in the development of free expression. On the other hand, Congress passed the Alien and Sedition Acts in 1798, and judges in both national and state courts persisted in applying the common law precedents of criminal and seditious libel. In the twentieth century, Congress has outlawed specific kinds of expression in the sedition section of the Espionage Act of 1917–1918 and by the Smith Act of 1940.

The First Amendment to the Constitution is central to any discussion of free speech in the United States. Despite the imperative and unequivocal nature of its language, a controversy of long standing has raged over what James Madison and the other framers of the First Amendment intended and over how it should be interpreted in light of our national experience and in view of contemporary conditions. John H. Kelly, in the second article of Part I, outlines three schools of thought on the problem of how the amendment should be interpreted.

One school of thought, reflected in early judicial opinions on freedom of speech and press, holds that the First Amendment was not intended to chart any new dimensions for freedom of expression, but rather was designed merely to declare the law as it existed in 1791. According to this view, the First Amendment was only meant to eliminate prior restraint and censorship. It did not modify the common law on criminal and seditious libel, nor did it prevent Congress from passing legislation restricting speech and press.

A second school maintains that the First Amendment was intended to abolish all prior restraints, to displace the common law precedents of seditious libel, and also to restrict the power of Congress to infringe on freedom of speech and press. It does contemplate civil actions for personal libel suits, however, and would permit legislation that could lead to criminal prosecution for expression inciting to a breach of the peace or that would pose an immediate threat to a substantial societal interest. While insisting on a wide latitude for speech and press activities, the advocates of this view nevertheless concede that there are limits to expression and that on occasions other values may take precedence. This interpretation of the First Amendment has undoubtedly been the dominant view of the Supreme Court in the past four and a half decades, and it has the support of such outstanding scholars as Zechariah Chafee. In contrast to the first school of thought, this approach distinguishes between verbal or written expression and overt action. Generally, freedom of expression would prevail except when it became closely associated or commingled with overt action of an illegal nature.

A third school of thought holds that freedom of expression may not be infringed under any circumstances; only overt actions may be punished. This is the absolutist's view of the First Amendment which appears to be the position of Justice Hugo Black, who more than once has expressed the opinion that the First Amendment was intended to forbid Congress from passing any legislation whatsoever that abridged freedom of speech and freedom of the press. In *Dennis v. United States* (1951), for instance, he would have held the Smith Act unconstitutional on its face, because its provision banning advocacy of violent overthrow of government infringed upon freedom of speech and press. The absolutist view of the First Amendment is reflected also in the work of Alexander Meiklejohn, who, nonetheless, draws a distinction between regulation and abridgement of free expression. Government may properly regulate the time, place, and conditions under which the right to speech may be exercised, but regulation may never be carried to the point of suppressing discussion of public concerns, regardless of their nature. While both Black and Meiklejohn would admit that the words of the First Amendment need some degree of interpretation, it is quite clear that in their view freedom of expression would approach the status of an absolute right.

Development of Constitutional Doctrine

While these three approaches provide a general orientation to the First Amendment, the Supreme Court has found them insufficiently precise as standards for disposing of cases coming before it. Consequently, the Court has supplemented these three schools of thought by various legal doctrines and tests designed to aid judges in the difficult task of deciding specific cases. The old doctrine handed down from the common law and the one that dominated judicial thinking until recent decades was the "bad tendency" test. According to this standard, government could suppress any expression that had a tendency to cause an injury to some interest government had a right to protect. The last major case in which this doctrine was used was *Gitlow v. New York,* decided in 1925. Here the Supreme Court of the United States declared that there was no question but that a "State in the exercise of its police powers may punish those who abuse this freedom of speech by utterances inimical to the public welfare, tending to corrupt public morals, incite to crime, or disturb the public peace. . . ." Note that what was said or published would not have to have an immediate effect of being inimical to public welfare or corrupting public morals or inciting to crime or disturbing the peace; it was enough to justify punishment if the words might tend to produce one of these evils some time in the future. The bad-tendency test is a product of the first school of thought mentioned above and as a practical matter offers virtually no protection to freedom of speech or press.

Consequently, it was a significant event in the history of free speech when Justice Oliver Wendell Holmes enunciated the "clear and present danger" doctrine in the *Schenck* case of 1919 (reprinted below as the opening selection of Part II). According to the new standard, "The question in every case is whether the words used are used in such circumstances and are of such a nature as to create evils that Congress has a right to prevent." Notice that there are distinct elements to the test. First, words alone, regardless of how inflammatory they may be, are not enough to justify

suppression. Rather, the words must be judged in the circumstances
in which they are used, and, together, the words and the circumstances must add up to a clear and "present," meaning an immediate, danger. Furthermore, the danger must be to an interest that
Congress has a right to protect. During the 1920's this doctrine
was further elaborated by Justices Holmes and Brandeis, often in
separate and dissenting opinions, and emerged as a challenge to,
and eventually displaced, the bad-tendency test. While the Holmes-
ian formula would permit suppression of speech under certain
circumstances, it opened up a far greater range for speech and
press than was possible under the old precedents.

The clear-and-present-danger test has been perhaps the most
famous of all constitutional doctrines; yet it has had a troubled
history. Certainly it has evoked an enormous amount of commen-
tary from all quarters, from those who think it goes too far in
protecting freedom of speech as well as from those who contend
that it does not go far enough. As a legal standard, it has been
condemned for failing to give sufficiently clear guidelines to the
policeman, to the prosecutor, and to the trial judge. In the succeeding two selections, Edward Hudon provides a friendly review
of the danger doctrine, while Walter Berns is highly critical of
both the philosophical basis and the practical application of the
doctrine.

The clear-and-present-danger doctrine did not reach its maturity
or command a majority of the Supreme Court until the 1940's, and
even then it flowered in conjunction with another constitutional
doctrine, the preferred-position approach to the First Amendment.
The supporters of this approach believed that the rights protected
by the First Amendment, especially freedom of speech, should be
accorded high priority in the ranking of constitutional values.
While First Amendment rights were not regarded as absolute, a
distinct preference for freedom was expressed and any restrictions
thereon would be closely scrutinized. The presumption, then, was
in favor of freedom of expression, and the only time it could be
otherwise was upon a showing that a clear and present danger to
a substantial interest would result from unrestrained speech or
press. Mr. Justice Rutledge's opinion in *Thomas v. Collins,* "A
Preference for First Amendment Freedoms," is followed by the
biting criticism of Mr. Justice Frankfurter, who, in turn, is taken
to task by Robert B. McKay. Whether or not it was a "mischievous
phrase," as Justice Frankfurter chose to label it, the preferred-

position doctrine, when linked with the clear-and-present-danger doctrine in the era of the Roosevelt Court, provided the high water mark for freedom of expression.

In the 1950's, the cold war, fear of internal subversion, and McCarthyism set in motion forces that tended to restrict freedom of expression. Under the leadership of Justice Frankfurter, the Supreme Court assumed a stance under which the preferred-position approach gave way to an approach requiring the *ad hoc* balancing of interests, and the clear-and-present-danger doctrine was displaced by the "gravity of the evil" test. Paul G. Kauper describes and defends this shift in Part II's seventh selection.

During the prosecution of communists under the Smith Act, the defendants contended that their First Amendment rights to freedom of speech, press, and association were involved; consequently, the government would have to prove that their activities created a clear and present danger of violent overthrow of the United States in order to gain a conviction. Certainly freedom of speech, press, and association were being infringed, and in all candor, the Justice Department would have had considerable difficulty in proving to a dispassionate forum that those "miserable merchants of unwanted wares," as Justice Douglas called the communists, posed an immediate threat to the continued existence of the United States Government. But the conviction of the American communists was sustained in *Dennis v. United States* (1951). In this case, the Supreme Court accepted a new standard for determining the scope of the First Amendment. This new standard was "the gravity of the evil," or the clear-and-*probable*-danger test. According to this formula, when the danger or evil that Congress is trying to prevent is sufficiently serious, such as violent overthrow of the government, the Justice Department does not have to prove that the danger is immediate. In the words of Chief Justice Vinson, the government need not wait "until the putsch is about to be executed"; rather it need only prove that the objective of the communists is violent overthrow of the government and that they intend to accomplish this evil deed "as speedily as circumstances would permit."

The shift to the "gravity of the evil" as the test for interpreting the First Amendment permitted convictions under the Smith Act which would have been difficult, if not impossible, with the clear-and-present-danger doctrine.

The impact of the *Dennis* case was softened somewhat by the decision of the Supreme Court in *Yates v. United States,* 1957. The critical point here was the interpretation of the term "advocacy" in the Smith Act. Justice Harlan explained that the kind of advocacy prohibited was that which called for overt illegal action, but that advocacy of Marxism-Leninism as a philosophy or as a view of history or as a system of values could not be suppressed. The effect of this decision was to increase the burden of proof placed upon the government; however, the Court did not overrule or abandon the "gravity of the evil" test, which presumably is still the standard of interpreting the First Amendment in relevant cases.

Justice Hugo Black has been the chief critic of the balance-of-interest test. In his now famous James Madison Lecture at the New York University Law School, he set forth his view that the First Amendment was intended to be and should be interpreted as prohibiting Congress from passing any legislation that "abridges" freedom of speech. In various opinions and especially in a 1962 public interview before the American Jewish Congress, Justice Black has continued his vigorous campaign for the primacy of the First Amendment freedoms. His position is spelled out in "Plain Words and Constitutional Absolutes." Although Black's absolute test would definitely expand the range of free expression and provide a more concrete meaning to constitutional rights, yet unexpected and serious consequences may result from his approach. Professor Sidney Hook caustically points out that, among other things, a man's right to a fair trial may be prejudiced by unrestrained freedom of the press.

Contemporary Problems

Professor Hook notwithstanding, there are indications that the Supreme Court is moving toward the absolute position suggested by Meiklejohn and Justice Black. In the Court's opinion on *New York Times v. Sullivan* (1964) (the opening selection of Part III) Justice Brennan speaks of the profound commitment to the "principle that debate on public issues should be uninhibited, robust, and wide-open. . . ." In this case, the newspaper was charged with libeling a public official in Alabama. The protection provided by the First Amendment is broad enough, maintained Brennan, to cover "vehement, caustic and sometimes unpleasantly sharp attacks on government and public officials" and even statements of factual error and defamations provided no actual malice is shown. Such a policy seems to eliminate the threat of the charge of seditious libel and to provide a clearer rationale for the earlier decision in the *Yates* case, in which the Court had held that the Smith Act could not be interpreted to ban the discussion or teaching of Marxism-Leninism. Noticeably absent from recent decisions are qualifying statements about clear and present danger or the need to balance competing interests. These would appear to be hopeful signs for those who maintain that the First Amendment should provide absolute protection for political discourse.

Professor Harry Kalven of the University of Chicago Law School, in Part III's second selection, professes to see the possibility of just such an approach to the First Amendment in the *New York Times* decision. In the process of absolving the newspaper of libel the Court held that the old Alien and Sedition Acts of 1798 were unconstitutional. Kalven sees this as a hopeful development, for he argues that the true meaning of freedom of speech has to be understood in reference to the crime of seditious libel. In his view:

. . . the absence of seditious libel as a crime is the true pragmatic test of freedom of speech. This I would argue is what freedom of speech is about. Any society in which seditious libel is a crime is . . . not a free society. A society can, for example, either treat obscenity as a crime or not treat it as a crime without thereby altering its basic nature as a society. It seems to me it cannot do so with seditious libel. Here the response to this crime defines the society.[1]

Apparently Kalven, like Brennan, would like to discard all the old verbiage such as clear and present danger, balancing of interests and the like, and start anew with the basic proposition that we are absolutely free to criticize government. His position is closely related to that espoused by Professor Alexander Meiklejohn and Justice Black who maintain that the First Amendment categorically prohibits infringements upon political discourse.

While this new formula would provide a firm constitutional basis for deciding purely free-speech and free-press cases, it may not be entirely appropriate for the increasing number of incidents where issues of free expression are mixed with overt forms of action. Consider, for example, the incident in Ann Arbor in which a group of students from the University of Michigan protested our involvement in the Viet Nam war by occupying the offices of the local draft board and disrupting, at least temporarily, the functions of that agency. In response, Selective Service authorities proceeded

[1] Harry Kalven, *The Negro and the First Amendment,* (Columbus, 1965), p. 16.

to reclassify as 1-A those demonstrators who had student deferments. Did this action raise First Amendment issues? Were the
students being punished for expressing their opposition to Selective
Service policies and to the war? Judge Medina, speaking for the
United States Court of Appeals for the Second Circuit, in "Students have Constitutional Rights Too," held that they were. Attorneys Schiesser and Benson follow with the argument that the draft
boards had acted within their range of discretion and that freedom
of expression was not involved.

Although favorable to the First Amendment claim, Judge Medina's
decision seems to have been made on an *ad hoc* basis without clear
guidelines for future controversies. The difficulty in deriving consistent constitutional doctrine from these situations is reflected in
a recent case involving a Negro student protest in front of a jail
in Florida. This protest was much like the one mentioned earlier
at the state capitol of South Carolina, yet in the concluding selection, Justice Black, a strong advocate of free speech, wrote an opinion denying that First Amendment issues were involved and upholding the conviction of the demonstrators.

The debate over the meaning and application of the First
Amendment goes on; however, the matter is not exclusively in
the hands of judges, lawyers, and prosecuting attorneys. Actually
only a fragment of the total confrontation reaches the formal stage
of court decision. In the larger sense, the true meaning of freedom
of expression is determined by the willingness of people to tol-
erate dissent, to be open-minded, to entertain new ideas, and to
submit their most cherished values to the test of comparison and
evaluation. On the other hand, those who challenge the existing
order by proposing new methods for handling problems or by
advocating new systems of values must consider the interests of
those adversely affected. It is within this broader social and political context that the real conflict between freedom of expression
and other societal interests must be worked out. The wisdom and
statesmanship we bring to the problem, both individually and col-
lectively, will be important in determining the viability and quality
of our political system.

I Historical Antecedents

AN ENGLISH HERITAGE

LEONARD W. LEVY

A Tradition of Suppression

Freedom of speech and stern measures for the suppression of dissent are both a part of our English heritage. Leonard W. Levy, historian and Dean of the Graduate School, Brandeis University, reviews the uncertain beginnings of free expression and notes its halting evolution under the challenges embodied in the structure of royal law.

WE KNOW VERY LITTLE . . . about the original understanding of the First Amendment's provision that "Congress shall make no law . . . abridging the freedom of speech, or of the press . . ." The meaning of no other clause of the Bill of Rights at the time of its framing and ratification has been so obscure to us. Historians, whether libertarian or not, have taken for granted that the Framers meant one thing or another, without inquiring into the evidence. One can do wonders with "insights" and inferences, depending upon one's predilections, but clear and preponderant proof has not been offered to elevate past generalizations beyond the level of a guess.

The sources, particularly for the period 1787–1791, are unfortunately almost silent on the matter under inquiry. The reason for the scantiness of the evidence goes far to explain why it is so difficult to ascertain the Framers' understanding of freedom of speech. That freedom had almost no history as a concept or a

Reprinted by permission of the publishers from Leonard W. Levy, *Legacy of Suppression,* pp. 4–15, Cambridge, Mass.: The Belknap Press of Harvard University Press, Copyright, 1960, by the President and Fellows of Harvard College.

practice prior to the First Amendment or even later. It developed as an offshoot of freedom of the press, on the one hand, and on the other, freedom of religion—the freedom to speak openly on religious matters. But as an independent concept referring to a citizen's personal right to speak his mind, freedom of speech was a very late development, virtually a new concept without basis in everyday experience and nearly unknown to legal and constitutional history or to libertarian thought on either side of the Atlantic prior to the First Amendment. The very phrase, "freedom of speech," until the last quarter of the eighteenth century referred primarily to a parliamentary, not a civil, right: the legislator's immunity from punishment for anything said by him in his official capacity during a legislative session. The phrase originated in Anglo-American history in the struggle of Parliament to achieve the privilege of free debate, and in that sense it has a history separate from the history of free speech as a civil liberty.

Freedom of speech could not become a civil liberty until the truth of men's opinions, especially their religious opinions, was regarded as relative rather than absolute; until kings and parliaments were sufficiently strong and stable to be able to ignore political criticism; and until the people were considered the source of sovereignty, the masters rather than the servants of the government. There could be no toleration of dissent when Catholics, Anglicans, and Puritans were profoundly convinced that the precise shade of belief which each respectively professed must be established as England's only true religion and that all be compelled to accept it for their own salvation as well as for the good of God and the nation. Heresy and nonconformity were severely prosecuted as crimes from the time the Inquisition was introduced in England and continued as crimes after the nationalization of the church under Henry VIII. Whether the government was Catholic or Protestant, Anglican or Puritan, the compulsion of conscience for the sake of uniformity necessitated restraints on freedom of speech and press regarding religion. The Reformation, moreover, by making the monarch the head of the established church, converted every religious question to a political one and suffused government policies with religious overtones. As a result, nonconformity and heresy became virtually indistinguishable from sedition and treason. Criticism of the church affected the state and vice versa. Not only was criticism dangerous; it was necessarily wrong when emanating from inferior subjects against their masters.

The danger was particularly great for several centuries after the emergence of the national state, when the life of the monarch was in jeopardy and the peace and security of the state were precarious. Freedom of religious and political expression was feared as a means of triggering conspiracies, internal disorders, wars, revolutions, or some other disastrous train of events that might pull down church and state.

Just as many torts or private wrongs became crimes, or offenses against the king's peace, so too certain libels, once only civilly redressable, became the objects of criminal retribution. As early as 1275 Parliament outlawed "any false news or tales whereby discord or occasion of discord or slander may grow between the king and his people or the great men of the realm . . ." The statute was reenacted in 1379 for the prevention of the "subversion and destruction of the said realm" by means of false speech.[1] Punishment was to be meted out by the king's council sitting in the "starred chamber." These were the earliest statutes making dangerous utterances a crime, and together with the ecclesiastical laws against heresy and other religious crimes they began the long history of the suppression of opinions deemed pernicious.

The invention of printing, of course, magnified the danger of such opinions. The crown claimed an authority to control printing presses as a right of prerogative. A system for the censorship of heretical manuscripts, long established by the English church and approved by Parliament, was taken over by Henry VIII and soon applied by him to writings on any subject. The manuscript of any work intended for publication had to be submitted to crown officials empowered to censor objectionable passages and to approve or deny a license for the printing of the work. Anything published without an *imprimatur* was criminal. Under Elizabeth the system of prior restraints upon the press was elaborately worked out, with the administration of the complex licensing system divided between three crown agencies: the Stationers Company, a guild of master publishers chartered to monopolize the presses and vested with extraordinary powers of search and seizure; the Court of High Commission, the highest ecclesiastical tribunal, which controlled the Stationers Company and did the actual licensing; and the Court of Star Chamber which issued the decrees defining crim-

---

[1] Van Vechten Veeder, "History of the Law of Defamation," in *Select Essays in Anglo-American Legal History,* comp. and ed. by a Committee of the Association of American Law Schools (Boston, 1909), 3:453–454.

inal matter and shared with the Court of High Commission jurisdiction over the trial of offenders. The agencies for enforcement
changed during the Puritan Revolution, but the licensing system
continued. Under the Restoration, the system was based principally
on an act of Parliament, rather than royal prerogative; it continued
until 1694. But the expiration of the system at that time did not
remotely mean that the press had become free. It was still subject
to the restraints of the common law.

One might publish without a license, but he did so at the peril
of being punished for libel. The point of departure for the modern
law of criminal libels was Sir Edward Coke's report of a Star
Chamber case of 1606, in which the following propositions were
stated. A libel against a private person might be punished crimi-
nally on the theory that it provokes revenge and therefore tends,
however remotely, to a breach of the peace. But a libel against a
government official is an even greater offense "for it concerns not
only the breach of the peace, but also the scandal of government . . ."[2] The essence of the crime as fixed by the medieval
statutes was the falsity of the libel, but the Star Chamber ruled
in 1606 that truth or falsity was not material, and ruled too that
the common-law courts also possessed jurisdiction over criminal
libels.

Four major classes of criminal libel emerged from subsequent
decisions in the common-law courts. Blasphemous libel, together
with laws against heresy and the establishment of a state church,
made freedom of expression on matters of religion a risk. The law
of obscene or immoral libel crimped literary, artistic, and other
forms of personal expression. So did the law of private libel which
protected individual reputations by making possible civil suits for
damages; but a private libel could also be prosecuted by the state
to prevent supposed bad tendencies to a breach of the peace. By
far the most repressive class of libel, however, was seditious libel.
It can be defined in a quite elaborate and technical manner in
order to take into account the malicious or criminal intent of the
accused, the bad tendency of his remarks, and their truth or falsity.
But the crime has never been satisfactorily defined, the necessary
result of its inherent vagueness. Seditious libel has always been
an accordion-like concept. Judged by actual prosecutions, the crime
consisted of criticizing the government: its form, constitution, offi-

---

[2] *De Libellis Famosis*, 3 Coke's *Reports* 254 (1606), quoted in Sir James Fitzjames Stephen,
A History of the Criminal Law of England (London, 1883), 2:304–305.

cers, laws, symbols, conduct, policies, and so on. In effect, any comment about the government which could be construed to have the bad tendency of lowering it in the public's esteem or of disturbing the peace was seditious libel, subjecting the speaker or writer to criminal prosecution.

Underlying the concept of seditious libel was the notion, expressed by Chief Justice Holt in Tuchin's case (1704), that "a reflection on the government" must be punished because, "If people should not be called to account for possessing the people with an ill opinion of the government, no government can subsist. For it is very necessary for all governments that the people should have a good opinion of it."[3] Through the seventeenth century, certain seditious libels which were construed as revealing an intention to "compass" or imagine the death of the king were punished as treason. In 1663, for example, William Twyn, for printing a book that endorsed the right of revolution, was held to have compassed the king's death; Twyn was sentenced to be hanged, cut down while still alive, and then emasculated, disemboweled, quartered, and beheaded—the standard punishment for treason. Algernon Sidney also paid the penalty for treason; his offense was the writing of an unpublished treatise on government discovered in his study. Treason as a purely verbal crime, unconnected with some overt act beyond the words themselves, died out after the execution of Mathews in 1720, convicted under a special statute rather than at common law. Utterances once held to be treasonable became wholly assimilated within the concept of seditious libel. As a lesser crime or misdemeanor, seditious libel was punished less severely: by imprisonment, fines, the pillory, and whipping. But prosecution for seditious libel became the government's principal instrument for controlling the press; according to Professor Siebert's excellent study of freedom of the press in England, "convictions for seditious libel ran into the hundreds" in both the seventeenth and eighteenth centuries.[4]

The procedure in prosecuting a seditious libel was even more objectionable, in the minds of the libertarian theorists, than the fact that the accused could be punished for words alone. From 1662 until a century later the secretary of state possessed the power of ferreting out seditious libels by issuing warrants which

[3] Rex v. Tuchin, Howell's *State Trials*, 14:1095, 1128 (1704), quoted in Stephen, *History of the Criminal Law in England*, 2:318.

[4] Siebert, *Freedom of the Press*, p. 365.

authorized a search of the homes and offices of all suspects and
the arrest of anyone on the mere suspicion of being implicated in
the writing, publishing, or circulation of such libels. General warrants, whose use was severely restricted in felony cases, were employed promiscuously in cases of seditious libel, a misdemeanor.
Search, seizure, and arrest were used as a means of harassing anti-
administration writers and editors against whom the evidence might
not warrant a trial. But the government was not restricted to trying only those indicted or presented by a grand jury. The attorney-
general might proceed against all misdemeanors by an information, that is, by determining the libelous character of a publication,
bringing it to the attention of the Court of the King's Bench, and
securing a warrant for the arrest and trial of the offender. Prosecuting by information rather than by indictment bypassed the
Englishman's beloved institution, the grand jury, which in felony
cases stood between him and the government. At the trial of a
seditious libel, the defendant was not even judged by his peers
in any meaningful way. Despite the ambiguity of earlier practice
the judges in the eighteenth century permitted juries to decide
only the fact of the publication. That is, the only question which
the jury passed upon was whether the defendant did or did not
publish the remarks charged against him and whether they carried
the innuendo as alleged. The judges reserved exclusively for themselves as a matter of law the decision on the crucial question
whether the defendant's remarks were maliciously intended and
of a bad tendency. The judges also refused to permit the defendant to plead the truth as a defense. Indeed, they proceeded
on the theory that the truth of a libel made it even worse because it was more provocative, thereby increasing the tendency
to breach of the peace or exacerbating the scandal against the
government. As a result of these rules applicable to criminal or
crown libels, a man might be arrested on a general warrant, prosecuted on an information without the consent of a grand jury, and
convicted for his political opinions by judges appointed by the
government he had aspersed.

Thus the disappearance of the prior restraints which had been
imposed by the licensing system until 1694 did not meaningfully
free the press. Theoretically one might say or print what he
pleased, but he was responsible to the common law for allegedly
malicious, scurrilous, scandalous, or derogatory utterances which
supposedly tended towards the contempt, ridicule, hatred, scorn,

or disrepute of other persons, religion, government, or morality. Blackstone, the oracle of the common law in the minds of the American Framers, summarized the law of crown libels as follows:

where blasphemous, immoral, treasonable, schismatical, seditious, or scandalous libels are punished by the English law . . . the liberty of the press, properly understood, is by no means infringed or violated. The *liberty of the press* is indeed essential to the nature of a free state; but this consists in laying no *previous* restraints upon publications, and not in freedom from censure for criminal matter when published. Every free-man has an undoubted right to lay what sentiments he pleases before the public: to forbid this is to destroy the freedom of the press: but if he publishes what is improper, mischievous, or illegal, he must take the consequences of his own temerity. . . . But to punish (as the law does at present) any dangerous or offensive writings, which, when published, shall on a fair and impartial trial be adjudged of a pernicious tendency, is necessary for the preservation of peace and good order, a government and religion, the only solid foundations of civil liberty. Thus the will of individuals is still left free; the abuse only of that free-will is the object of legal punishment. Neither is any restraint hereby laid upon free-dom of thought or enquiry: liberty of private sentiment is still left; the disseminating, or making public, of bad sentiments, destructive of the ends of society, is the crime which society corrects.[5]

The common law's definition of freedom of the press meant merely the absence of censorship in advance of publication. But the presence of punishment afterwards, for "bad sentiments," oral or published, had an effect similar to a law authorizing previous restraints. A man who may be whipped and jailed for what he says or prints is not likely to feel free to express his opinions even if he does not need a government license to do so. The common-law definition of freedom of the press left the press at the mercy of the crown's prosecutors and judges. Freedom of dis-cussion and the law of libel were simply incompatible; the first could not coexist with the second.

[5] Sir William Blackstone, *Commentaries on the Laws of England* (London, 1765–1769), Book 4, ch. 11, pp. 151–152; or, in the 18th ed., which I used (New York, 1836), 2:112–113.

JOHN H. KELLY

The Common Law, Sedition, and the First Amendment

John H. Kelly, a graduate of Yale Law School, is associated with Milbank, Tweed, Hope, and Hadley, a New York City law firm. As his article below points out, the problem of determining the limits of political discourse is not new to Americans. The trial of Peter Zenger in 1735, the adoption of the First Amendment in 1791, and the passage of the Alien and Sedition Acts in 1798 are historical landmarks in the continuing debate over the boundaries of free expression.

THE AMERICAN REVOLUTION was one manifestation of the great democratic movement of the 18th century, which began to see a new concept of government accepted and applied by the western world. The traditional view, that the ruler was master of the people and, by virtue of his position, beyond any reproach which might lessen his authority, gave way to the belief that the ruler was the servant of a people who guided their own destinies through his agency. Under this philosophy there could be no such offense as seditious libel; there could be breaches of the peace and incitements to action which might endanger the security of a warring state, but, beyond these immediate harms to the whole state, the only result of critical speech would be the ouster of the discredited ruling body and the substitution of a new group of servants. In fact, a turnover of governments would indicate the responsiveness of the machinery of government to the hand of the people.

From John Kelly, "Criminal Libel and Free Speech," *Kansas Law Review* (1958), Vol. 6, pp. 305–316. Reprinted by permission of the *Kansas Law Review* and of the author.

But before this idea was made possible of practical acceptance by the victory at Yorktown, the King of England ruled America as master, and the English law of libel was imposed on colonists who, even more than their brothers in England, wished freedom to censure a government which permitted them no representation in the governing body. The colonists were denied adequate political voice, and the imposition of libel laws which bottled up popular criticism made armed revolution the only course open to aggrieved Americans. "It is probable that no one thing contributed more to enflame the public mind against the common law than did the insistence of the American courts on enforcing the harsh doctrines of the English law of criminal libel—that truth was no defense and that the jury could pass only on the fact of publication and the application of the innuendo."[1]

Colonial times were rife with a continuing struggle between the royal judges and the American writers and printers, who demanded freedom to criticize and whose counsel in trial after trial attempted to gain this freedom by asking greater rights for the jury. The culmination of this line of cases, which saw American publishers punished for censuring the King, Parliament and the colonial governors, was the celebrated trial of John Peter Zenger in New York in 1735.

Zenger's "Journal" was published in opposition to the royal organ, the "Gazette," and was the vehicle for vehement attacks on the colonial governors and government. The grand jury would not indict, but the Attorney General exhibited a paper charging Zenger with criminal libel, and, after eight months of imprisonment, he was brought to trial where he was defended by Andrew Hamilton, who was even then one of the most influential advocates of a free press. Hamilton could not deny the fact of publication, and the court wished the jury to bring back a special verdict on this issue, leaving to itself the question of the libelous tendency of the articles. But Hamilton asked the jury to witness the truth of what his client had said and to bring back a general verdict of not guilty, so as to secure "that to which nature and the laws of our country have given us a right—both of exposing and opposing arbitrary power (in these parts of the world at least) by speaking and writing truth."[2] In reply, Chief Justice James DeLancey denied the right of the defendant to prove truth, by charging the jury that

[1] Warren, *History of the American Bar* 236 (1st ed. 1913).

[2] 17 Howell's St. Tr. at 722.

"whether the words as set forth in the information make a libel; and that is a matter of law, no doubt, and which you may leave to the court."[3] The issue was joined; in spite of the charge, a general verdict would mean acquittal. The jury returned the general verdict of not guilty and the prisoner was released to the cheers of the spectators in the court, while through the colonies word went out of the victory of the press over the tyranny of oppressive law. The fact, noted by the compiler of the cases, that the doctrines advocated by Mr. Hamilton were not allowed in the courts as law, went unheard by the public. The interest in and approval of the outcome of the Zenger trial was a symptom of a revolutionary spirit which, nurtured by writers such as Zenger and Paine, was to sweep the country and lead to a revolution whose success would be as much due to the pamphleteer as to the minuteman. The Revolutionary and post-Revolutionary era was marked by the attempts of the newly independent colonists, influenced by their vivid memories of the oppressions of England and their recent support and applause of the radical writers, to preserve in their constitutional declarations the freedom of the press that had been so vital to the Revolution. The press could not be regarded as a tool of the ruling group in a democratic state. Under the democratic theory of government it had to take its place as the spokesman of the popular opinion which was to rule.

The great legal and historical question arising out of these original declarations of the freedom of speech is, to what extent did they modify the law existing before revolution had made their enactment possible? Although recent cases have rested their holdings on the varying conclusions of American judges as to the answer to this question, the historical evidence is unclear and the views of the legal historians conflicting.

A declaration of the First Continental Congress in 1774 enumerated the benefits of a free press, without which a people cannot be free:

. . . in the advancement of truth, science, morality, and arts in general, in its diffusion of liberal sentiments on the administration of government, the ready communication of thoughts between subjects, and the consequential promotion of union among them whereby oppressive officers are shamed or intimidated into more honorable and just modes of conducting affairs.[4]

[3] *Ibid.*
[4] Cited by Kent, J. in People v. Croswell, 3 Johns. 337, 391 (N.Y. 1804).

This statement sets forth what is essentially the modern view of the foundation of the freedom of the press, the necessity of the free flow of ideas about matters of public importance for the attainment of truth and responsive government. The Virginia Religious Liberty Statute of 1777 preserved the right of liberty of speech and recognized that mere words, unaccompanied by action, could not be punished. "It is time enough for the rightful purposes of civil government for its officers to interfere when principles break out into overt acts against peace and good order."[5] Such declarations clearly indicate the interest of their framers in preserving the right to political, i.e., public, criticism and imply that the limitation on such criticism should be its creation of actual violence.

The first constitutional declaration of the right of free speech and press was contained in the bill of rights drafted by George Mason in 1776 for the Virginia Constitution, and, by the opening of the Constitutional Convention in 1787, eleven states had such provisions embodied in their constitutions or bills of rights. Three of the early declarations are as follows:

Delaware: The press shall be free to every citizen who undertakes to examine the official conduct of men acting in a public capacity, and any citizen may print freely on any subject, being responsible for the abuse of that liberty. . . .

Massachusetts: The liberty of the press is essential to the security of freedom and that it ought not, therefore, to be restrained.

United States: Congress shall make no law respecting the establishment of religion, or prohibiting the free exercise thereof; or abridging the freedom of speech, or of the press; or the right of the people peaceably to assemble, and to petition the government for a redress of grievances.

There are three possible interpretations of these provisions. First, it may be contended that they preserve the freedom of speech as an absolute right which may not be abridged in any manner. Certainly the absolute phraseology of the United States provision lends support to this view, but this wording is misleading if it is allowed to take on the qualities of a "natural law" and is construed without consideration of the historical necessities of its creation and its natural implications. At present, only three state constitutions contain such an "absolute" provision. All others limit the

---

[5] Schofield, *Constitutional Law and Equity* at 522 (1921).

freedom of the press or of speech by some variation of the phrase making the publisher "responsible for the abuse of that liberty." The universality of such qualifying provisions indicates that they are implied in those constitutions lacking them. In addition, the thrust of the United States provision is slightly different from that of the states. The states were setting down the ultimate rule as to the extent of the freedom of speech. The Union, on the other hand, was merely denying the power of Congress to legislate in this area, leaving to the states the power to restrain speech as they saw fit. In other words, the U.S. Constitutional provision merely negatives the right of Congress to abridge speech; the states set forth in positive terms the right to speak freely, and in doing so, forty-five of them have found it necessary to limit free speech by making the publisher responsible for its abuse. Also, mention, in both state provisions cited, of the right of the "press," and the limitation in the Delaware declaration to citizens examining "the official conduct of men acting in a public capacity," indicate that an absolute "freedom of speech" was not intended, but rather a right limited to publications on matters of public import. This is borne out by the earlier declarations, as that of the Continental Congress, which talk in terms of discussions of science, the arts, government and politics as being in the area of speech deserving of protection. Essentially, such declarations imply that the freedom of speech exists because such freedom is of benefit to the public and that speech not benefiting the public, i.e., speech on matters of purely private concern, does not fall within the constitutionally protected area. The political and legal struggle for freedom of speech since the first opposition to the Star Chamber was manifestly directed at obtaining the right of political criticism, not of obtaining an absolute right to speak.

This problem of the proper interpretations of the absolute wording of these provisions was discussed by William Cushing, President of the Constitutional Convention of 1780, in correspondence with John Adams, the principal draftsman of the Bill of Rights, regarding the Massachusetts Constitution. Cushing, with whom Adams apparently agreed, noted that the provision was absolute in terms and that all publication seemed to be protected. He felt, however, that in spite of this mandate, the press had to be restrained from injuring the public or individuals by the propagation of falsehoods. He resolved this dilemma by stating that what was to be preserved was, in the words of the Constitution, that liberty of the press "essential to the security of freedom," and that that was the liberty of truthful public discussion which could never effectually injure a good government. When the press became the vehicle of scandal and falsehood, however, punishment was necessary and proper.

Thus the First Amendment, when looked at in terms of the historical necessities of its creation and in the light of other constitutional declarations, cannot be construed as an absolute protection of speech. It was fully appreciated that speech could be abused and that the state had no interest in certain areas of speech.

A second interpretation of the guarantees of free speech, one which stands at the opposite pole from that just discussed, is that "the constitutional guaranty in question was intended not only to abolish forever previous censorship of publications by the government, but also to safeguard the citizen from any larger liability for his uncensored publication, or for his public utterance, than was imposed by the rules of the common law as accepted at the time of the making of the federal constitution."[6] Under this view, which, as will be noted below, has gained wide judicial acceptance, the constitutional statements in question were merely declaratory of the law existing at the time of their enactment.

This theory is based on a realization of the extreme importance of the doctrine of prior restraint in Anglo-American jurisprudence and the belief that with the removal of this age-old device, men felt that freedom of the press had been obtained. The statements of free speech, in the constitutions of the new country, guaranteed that there could be no return to the censorship, but left intact the common law of criminal libel which was felt to be a necessary limitation on the freedom of speech. Any excesses in the application of the law of seditious libel were to be mitigated by expanding the role of the jury in such cases and by broadening the concept of privileged comment.

This doctrine is condemned by writers who espouse the third interpretation that the manifest purpose of these declarations was to repudiate the law of the colonial courts and to create a new and expanded, though not an absolute, freedom of the press. They point out that the censorship had expired in England in 1694 and in America in 1725 and that the framers of the constitutional declarations must have assumed that it was a now obsolete and outlawed manifestation of absolute rule. On the other hand, they

---

[6] Vance, *Freedom of Speech and of the Press,* 2 MINN. L. REV. 239, 255 (1917).

had real reason to fear seditious libel actions, which had been brought with renewed vigor after the decline of the censorship and which were painful memories to many of the framers themselves. In addition, the popular feeling of the 18th century, with its emphasis on the right of free discussion of political affairs and its vocal disapproval of the royal law applied in trials such as that of Zenger, indicates an intention to do away with the oppressive seditious libel doctrine. Under this view, both censorship and seditious libel are rejected, and prosecutions for criticism of the government, without direct incitement to law breaking, are made impossible in the United States. Restrictions on speech can be imposed as indicated above, but the freedom of political criticism was preserved.

This theory seems to the author to most accurately reflect what must have been the intention of the framers of the original declarations of the freedom of speech. However, even if the common man and his legislators fully believed that the law of seditious libel was stamped out by their efforts, the judges of the young nation unanimously disagreed, and American publishers suddenly found that censure of the government in power brought forth the same reaction that it had before the Revolution. Contemporary judicial opinion took the view that the constitutional provisions were only declaratory of the English common law as set down after the expiration of licensing in 1694. . . .

The theory that declarations of freedom of the press only forbade prior restraint and that subsequent punishment for seditious utterance was not barred, underlay the creation of the notorious Alien and Sedition Acts, which were widely regarded as declaratory of the then existing common law. The Sedition Act made punishable writing, publishing, or speaking anything "false, scandalous and malicious" against the administration, Congress or the President "with intent to defame . . . or to bring them . . . into contempt or disrepute . . . or to stir up sedition within the United States . . ." The third section of the act permitted the defendant to give, in defense, proof of the truth of his utterance, and gave the jury the right to determine "the law and the fact" under the direction of the court, as in other cases.

Assuming the validity of the contention that the First Amendment prohibits only prior restraint, the Sedition Act was hardly the pernicious legislation it is usually made out. It both restricted the scope of criminal libel and extended the defenses allowed in the libel action. Instead of the common law definition of seditious libel, which made intentional publication of written blame of public men or institutions a crime and enabled a judge to apply this definition by subjective judgment, the Sedition Act required intent to defame or to stir up sedition. This made the question of whether or not a libel had been committed an issue for the jury, and it made possible criticism which formerly would have been punishable on a mere judgment of its "tendency" by the court. It required that the utterance be false, and thus preserved the right of truthful criticism demanded by the Revolutionary pamphleteers and by Hamilton and his colleagues. In its third section, the Sedition Act made specific the right of the jury to try law and fact and the defense of truth, which were implied in the definition of the crime in section two. Therefore, if the populace only expected the Constitution to protect them from prior restraints, they would have gladly received an act which rejected the greater part of the common law seditious libel doctrine. The manifest opposition to the Alien and Sedition Acts was an important indication that the freedom of speech and the press had a much broader popular connotation than the mere prohibition of prior restraint.

Madison, supporting the Virginia and Kentucky resolutions which protested the Sedition Act, was a spokesman for this popular view:

> The freedom of the press, under the common law, is, in the defenses of the Sedition Act, made to consist in an exemption from all previous restraint on printed publications, by persons authorized to inspect or prohibit them. It appears to the committee that this idea of freedom of the press can never be admitted to be the American idea of it; since a law inflicting penalties on printed publications would have a similar effect with a law authorizing a previous restraint on them. It would seem a mockery to say that no laws should be passed preventing publications from being made, but that laws might be passed for punishing them in case they should be made.[7]

The constitutionality of the Acts was never tested as most state legislatures disagreed with the Virginia and Kentucky resolutions and affirmed the propriety and the necessity of the Acts. The thrust of the Constitutional debate was not that the legislation was an infringement on the right of speech, but that it was the exercise of a power not granted the Federal Government. In 1787, Charles

[7] Elliott, *Debates on the Federal Constitution* 569 (2d ed. 1866).

Pinckney proposed to the Philadelphia Convention that the Constitution contain a clause protecting the freedom of the press. He was voted down, in spite of the fact that eleven states had such clauses in their constitutions and bills of rights. The probable basis for this result was that the power of Congress did not extend to the press and so could never abridge it. However, popular pressure forced adoption of such a clause in 1791. The constitutional issue is moot, and neither the perspective of modern scholars nor the proximity of contemporary ones has made possible a certain answer of what the court should have done had the issue been raised. Probably the Act would today be unconstitutional as an infringement of First Amendment rights, though not as an exercise of undelegated power. What the early court would have done is fairly clear; judicial willingness to impose punishment under the Act and unwillingness to accept its mitigating doctrines indicates that it was regarded as valid and justifiable legislation.

Statistics on the Act are meager, but it has been estimated that at least 24 or 25 persons were arrested, 15 indicted, and 10 convicted for its infringement. The most familiar cases involved the conviction of four Republicans who had censured John Adams and his administration with the intent of arousing the people against the Adams government, thereby causing Jefferson to be elected. The publications were generally true on the facts or as opinions allowable from the facts, and nothing in them could be remotely construed as urging the use of arms or rebellion. However, convictions were obtained under the provisions of the Sedition Act, which the courts strictly applied. In the *Cooper* case, Justice Chase allowed proof of truth to be admitted, but charged: ". . . the traverser in his defense must prove every charge he has made to be true, he must prove it to the marrow. If he asserts three things and proves but two, he fails in his defense, for he must prove the whole of his assertions to be true."[8] While stating the rule that intent must be proved as any fact, Chase applied it to Cooper as follows: "This conduct showed that he (Cooper) intended to dare and defy the government, and to provoke them, and his subsequent conduct satisfies my mind that such was his disposition. For he justifies the publication in all its parts, and declares it to be founded in truth. It is proved most clearly to be his publication. It is your business to consider the intent as coupled with that, and view the whole together." The court came very close to assuming the prov-

[8] 25 Fed. Cas. at 642–43.

ince of the jury in judging intent, and the net result of these cases was the fining and imprisonment of citizens for political criticism which created no greater danger than the defeat of the Federalist party at the polls. Such actions denoted a reversion to the theory of government as master of the people, immune from censure. Chase admits this in the *Cooper* decision. "All governments which I have ever read or heard of punish libels against themselves. If a man attempts to destroy the confidence of the people in their officers, their supreme magistrates, and their legislature, he effectually saps the foundation of the government."

The Alien and Sedition Acts were exceedingly unpopular, though in view of Jefferson's narrow victory in 1800 it can hardly be said that the people rose up as a whole in righteous wrath against the despoilers of liberty. However, the Federalists did lose the Presidency and Congress, and it is generally felt that the Alien and Sedition Acts contributed largely to their downfall. The Acts had been designed to perpetuate Federalist control, and in this they failed, leaving a party whose philosophy was outmoded and whose popularity was destroyed. The American temper demanded a much broader freedom of speech than was permitted under the Sedition Act.

All persons convicted under the Act were pardoned by Jefferson and their fines repaid by the Congress. The significance of this gesture should not be overrated as the "libels" had been uttered for the benefit of the pardoning party, and the principal justification for the return of the fines was that the Act was deemed an intrusion by the Federal Government into a field reserved to the states. The Sedition Act expired in 1801.

The protest against the Act began to lay to rest the idea of a national common law of seditious libel, and in the states, prosecutions for seditious libel became so extremely unpopular that they became less and less frequent until officials ceased to invoke the doctrine and were remitted to their individual civil or criminal remedies. On the other hand, the opponents of the Act had to make some concessions, at least inferentially. The controversy resulted in the acceptance of the idea that the government did have the power to protect its fundamental interests and to prevent the counseling of disorder and lawbreaking. The enactment of this law by an administration desirous of maintaining its rule in the face of popular opposition brought to an issue the extent of the power of a democratic government to stifle criticism, and the ultimate failure of the Act proved that Americans believed that they had an indestructible right of political criticism.

In the years following the release of the publishers sentenced under the Sedition Act, seditious libel, as defined under the common law or under the Act, disappeared from American jurisprudence. Since then, the numerous laws which have been passed to control speech which directly affects the government have been phrased in non-libel terms. Their purpose and effect together with their relation to the First Amendment have in many instances been the same as the doctrines of seditious libel, but a consideration of these enactments is beyond the scope of this article. At any rate, these laws have been focused on speech which incites to action against the government rather than that which merely breeds ill-opinion of the ruling group, and legislators and judges upholding such laws have been careful not to mention "seditious libel," a phrase which must forever be connected with the Star Chamber, Judges Dana and Jeffries and the Alien and Sedition Acts.

II

The Supreme Court and the Uncertain Meaning of the First Amendment

THE CLEAR AND PRESENT DANGER DOCTRINE

MR. JUSTICE OLIVER WENDELL HOLMES

Marking the Limits of Free Speech: The Danger Test

Oliver Wendell Holmes had been an Associate Justice and was the Chief Justice of the Supreme Judicial Court of Massachusetts at the time of his appointment by President Theodore Roosevelt in 1902 to the U.S. Supreme Court. He served in that capacity for thirty years.

During World War I, Mr. Schenck circulated printed material which denounced the Selective Service Act and our participation in the European conflict. He was found guilty of violating the Espionage Act of 1917, and his conviction was appealed to the Supreme Court. Schenck v. United States (1919) is significant for at least two reasons. It marks the first time that the Supreme Court ruled on a claim that freedom of expression had been violated by an act of Congress, and it was the occasion on which Mr. Justice Holmes, speaking for the Court, announced the clear-and-present-danger doctrine.

THIS IS AN INDICTMENT in three counts. The first charges a conspiracy to violate the Espionage Act of June 15, 1917, by causing

Mr. Justice Holmes speaking for the Supreme Court in *Schenck v. United States,* 249 U. S. 47 (1919). Case citations omitted.

29

and attempting to cause insubordination, etc., in the military and naval forces of the United States, and to obstruct the recruiting and enlistment service of the United States, when the United States was at war with the German Empire; to wit, that the defendant wilfully conspired to have printed and circulated to men who had been called and accepted for military service under the Act of May 18, 1917, a document set forth and alleged to be calculated to cause such insubordination and obstruction. The count alleges overt acts in pursuance of the conspiracy, ending in the distribution of the document set forth.The second count alleges a conspiracy to commit an offense against the United States; to wit, to use the mails for the transmission of matter declared to be nonmailable by title 12, § 2, of the Act of June 15, 1917, to wit, the above-mentioned document, with an averment of the same overt acts. The third count charges an unlawful use of the mails for the transmission of the same matter and otherwise as above. The defendants were found guilty on all the counts. They set up the 1st Amendment to the Constitution, forbidding Congress to make any law abridging the freedom of speech or of the press, and, bringing the case here on that ground, have argued some other points also of which we must dispose.

The document in question, upon its first printed side, recited the 1st section of the 13th Amendment, said that the idea embodied in it was violated by the Conscription Act, and that a conscript is little better than a convict. In impassioned language it intimated that conscription was despotism in its worst form and a monstrous wrong against humanity, in the interest of Wall Street's chosen few. It said: "Do not submit to intimidation;" but in form at least confined itself to peaceful measures, such as a petition for the repeal of the act. The other and later printed side of the sheet was headed, "Assert Your Rights." It stated reasons for alleging that anyone violated the Constitution when he refused to recognize "your right to assert your opposition to the draft," and went on: "If you do not assert and support your rights, you are helping to deny or disparage rights which it is the solemn duty of all citizens and residents of the United States to retain." It described the arguments on the other side as coming from cunning politicians and a mercenary capitalist press, and even silent consent to the Conscription Law as helping to support an infamous conspiracy. It denied the power to send our citizens away to foreign shores to shoot up the people of other lands, and added that words could not express the condemnation such cold-blooded ruthlessness deserves, etc., etc., winding up, "You must do your share to maintain, support, and uphold the rights of the people of this country." Of course the document would not have been sent unless it had been intended to have some effect, and we do not see what effect it could be expected to have upon persons subject to the draft except to influence them to obstruct the carrying of it out. The defendants do not deny that the jury might find against them on this point.

But it is said, suppose that that was the tendency of this circular, it is protected by the 1st Amendment to the Constitution. Two of the strongest expressions are said to be quoted respectively from well-known public men. It well may be that the prohibition of laws abridging the freedom of speech is not confined to previous restraints, although to prevent them may have been the main purpose. . . . We admit that in many places and in ordinary times the defendants, in saying all that was said in the circular, would have been within their constitutional rights. But the character of every act depends upon the circumstances in which it is done. . . . The most stringent protection of free speech would not protect a man in falsely shouting fire in a theater, and causing a panic. It does not even protect a man from an injunction against uttering words that may have all the effect of force. . . . The question in every case is whether the words used are used in such circumstances and are of such a nature as to create a clear and present danger that they will bring about the substantive evils that Congress has a right to prevent. It is a question of proximity and degree. When a nation is at war many things that might be said in time of peace are such a hindrance to its effort that their utterance will not be endured so long as men fight, and that no court could regard them as protected by any constitutional right. . . .

Judgments affirmed.

EDWARD G. HUDON

The Danger Test in Retrospect

Edward G. Hudon is a former assistant librarian to the Supreme Court of the United States, and is presently an Assistant U.S. Attorney for Maine. In the selection below, he points out that there are distinct phases in the evolution of the clear-and-present-danger doctrine. He describes the initial development of the doctrine by Justices Holmes and Brandeis in cases growing out of the espionage and sedition acts of World War I and from state anti-syndicalism acts of the 1920's.

ALONG WITH AMERICAN PARTICIPATION in World War I came the Espionage Act cases which were convictions for violations of the Espionage Acts of 1917 and 1918. Most of these cases arose from violations of Title I, § 3, of the 1917 act as originally passed and as amended by the 1918 act. Some were finally disposed of during the war, others after the war had ended, but all were upheld with use-abuse or liberty versus license as the main prop.

As originally enacted, Title I, § 3, made it punishable for anyone, when the United States is at war, to willfully "make or convey false reports or false statements with the intent to interfere with the operation or success of the military or naval forces of the United States or to promote the success of its enemies;" to "willfully cause or attempt to cause insubordination, disloyalty, mutiny, or refusal of duty, in the military or naval forces of the United States;" or to "willfully obstruct the recruiting or enlistment service of the United States, to the injury of the service of the United States." The 1918 act left the 1917 act intact except that it added "attempts to obstruct the recruiting or enlistment service," plus nine other offenses.

The first noteworthy case, *Masses Publishing Co.* v. *Patten,* never went beyond the Court of Appeals. Nevertheless it set the pattern.

From Edward G. Hudon, *Freedom of Speech and Press in America* (1963), pp. 57–59, 70–75. Reprinted by permission of the Public Affairs Press and of the author.

It started out as a "direct incitement" case but it ended up as one that hinged on "bad tendency." The former was used by the lower court and the latter in the intermediate court. The case arose when the Postmaster of New York City excluded from the mails an issue of *The Masses,* a monthly revolutionary journal. The publication printed cartoons and text attacking the war which were considered objectionable under the provisions of the 1917 act declaring non-mailable any publication violating its criminal section. District Judge Learned Hand was appealed to by the publisher for a preliminary injunction against the postmaster which he granted.

In his opinion Judge Hand laid down rules that followed the "direct or indirect incitement" test. Outside of the boundaries of free speech he placed counsel or advice to others "to violate the law as it stands." "Words," he observed, "are not only the keys of persuasion, but the triggers of action, and those which have no purport but to counsel the violation of law cannot by any latitude of interpretation be a part of that public opinion which is the final source of government in a democratic state." Within the boundaries he placed conduct which "stops short of urging upon others that it is their duty or their interest to resist the law."

In summarizing his philosophy of free speech, Judge Hand declared: "Political agitation, by the passions it arouses or the convictions it engenders, may in fact stimulate men to the violation of law. Detestation of existing policies is easily transformed into forcible resistance of the authority which puts them in execution, and it would be folly to disregard the causal relation between the two. Yet to assimilate agitation, legitimate as such, with direct incitement to violent resistance, is to disregard the tolerance of all methods of political agitation which in normal times is a safeguard of free government. The distinction is not a scholastic subterfuge, but a hard-bought acquisition in the fight for freedom, and the purpose to disregard it must be evident when the power exists."[1]

Judge Hand was reversed not on his determination of what speech is or is not protected, but on a principle of administrative law. By the provisions of the act, whether or not something is mailable must be determined by the Postmaster in the exercise of his judgment and discretion; his decision is conclusive and cannot be reversed by the courts unless it is clearly wrong. Nevertheless, for good measure the Court of Appeals threw out Judge Hand's determination of free speech and substituted "bad tendency." "If,"

[1] 244 Fed. 535, 540 (D.C., S.D., N.Y., 1917).

it held, "the natural and reasonable effect of what is said is to encourage resistance to a law, and the words are used in an endeavor to persuade to resistance, it is immaterial that the duty to resist is not mentioned, or the interest of the persons addressed in resistance is not suggested."

The first of the Espionage Act cases to reach the Supreme Court of the United States was *Schenck* v. *United States*. Schenck, the defendant, had attended to the printing and distributing of leaflets which advocated opposition and resistance to the World War I draft. He had done this in his capacity as general secretary of the Socialist Party. The prohibitions of the First Amendment against infringement of speech and press were set up as a defense. A unanimous Court upheld the conviction with an opinion written by Mr. Justice Holmes in which he launched his classic "clear and present danger" test. "The question in every case," he wrote, "is whether the words used are used in such circumstances and are of such a nature as to create a clear and present danger that they will bring about the substantive evils that Congress has a right to prevent." At this point, however, the now famous test had not yet matured. It was still but an embryo. Although it provided a more liberal tone to what had already been said on the subject of speech and press, it was still coupled with "bad intent" and "bad tendency." Thus wrote the Justice: "If the act (speaking, or circulating a paper), its tendency and intent with which it is done are the same, we perceive no ground for saying that success alone warrants making the act a crime."

Seven days after his opinion in the *Schenck* case, Justice Holmes delivered unanimous opinions in the *Frohwerk* and the *Debs* cases in which two more convictions for violations of the Espionage Act were upheld. In neither of these did Holmes avail himself of the opportunity to elaborate on his "clear and present danger" test. Zechariah Chafee once suggested that perhaps Holmes was waiting for a more opportune moment and a decision that he considered clearly wrong. Chafee pointed out that as it happened Holmes could launch his novel theory with the backing of a unanimous Court, something that he could not have done otherwise. Consequently, Chafee was of the opinion that freedom of speech profited more as a result than if Holmes had voted for a reversal. This is interesting in the light of comments which Holmes made on the *Debs* case in two of his letters to Pollock.

In his letter of April 5, 1919, Holmes wrote to Pollock: "I am beginning to get stupid letters of protest against a decision that Debs, a noted agitator, was rightly convicted of obstructing the recruiting service so far as the law was concerned. I wonder that the Government should press the case to a hearing before us, as the inevitable result was that fools, knaves, and ignorant persons were bound to say he was convicted because he was a dangerous agitator and that obstructing the draft was a pretence. How it was with the Jury of course I don't know, but of course that talk is silly as to us. There was a lot of jaw about free speech, which I dealt with somewhat summarily in an earlier case—*Schenck* v. *U. S.* . . . also *Frohwerk* v. *U. S.* . . . As it happens I should go farther probably than the majority in favor of it, and I daresay it was partly on that account that the C.[hief]J.[ustice] assigned the case to me."[2]

In his letter of April 27, 1919, Holmes wrote further: "Of course there were people who pitched into the Court for sending Debs to prison under the espionage act, but there was no doubt that the jury was warranted in finding him guilty or that the act was Constitutional. Now I hope the President will pardon him and some other poor devils with whom I have more sympathy. Those whose cases have come before us have seemed to me poor fools whom I should have been inclined to pass over if I could. The greatest bores in the world are the come-outers who are cocksure of a dozen nostrums. The dogmatism of a little education is hopeless."[3]

If what Holmes was waiting for was a more opportune moment he apparently found it in *Abrams* v. *United States*. Here he expressed his views by way of dissent, unhampered by any fear that one of the "vital organs" would be cut from his opinion. By his own admission, it was in this dissent that he intended to set out the full limits of "clear and present danger" as he meant it.

After a recitation of the circumstances of the distribution of the two pamphlets that formed the basis of the indictment and a description of the inflammatory nature of their contents, the Justice started his discussion of the law with an elaboration of the meaning of "intent." He recognized that as vaguely used in ordinary legal discussion, "intent" means knowledge of the facts at the time an act is committed from which common experience indicates that certain consequences will follow, whether or not foreseen by the actor. But he drew a distinction where words are used exactly, and

[2] *Pollock-Holmes Letters,* v. 2, p. 7.
[3] *Ibid.,* p. 11.

the statute had to be taken to use its words in a strict and accurate sense. He wrote: "a deed is not done with intent to produce a consequence unless that consequence is the aim of the deed." In other words, actual intent is necessary. He reaffirmed that the *Schenck, Frohwerk* and *Debs* cases were correctly decided, and then he continued:

"I do not doubt for a moment that by the same reasoning that would justify punishing persuasion to murder, the United States constitutionally may punish speech that produces or is intended to produce a clear and imminent danger that it will bring about forthwith certain substantive evils that the United States constitutionally may seek to prevent. The power undoubtedly is greater in time of war than in time of peace because war opens dangers that do not exist at other times.

"But as against dangers peculiar to war, as against others, the principle of the right to free speech is always the same. It is only the present danger of immediate evil or an intent to bring it about that warrants Congress in setting a limit to the expression of opinion where private rights are not concerned. Congress certainly cannot forbid all effort to change the mind of the country."[4]

Actual intent Holmes considered essential where a further act of the actor is required to complete the substantive crime, or where success depends on the acts of others. Indeed, the actor's aim might be brought about, but without the evil sought to be checked. And in this case an intent to prevent interference in Russia might have been satisfied without provoking resistance to the war effort of the United States against Germany. Abrams, Holmes felt, was guilty of expressing opinions and exhortations privileged by the Constitution. He defended this privilege as follows:

"Persecution for the expression of opinions seems to me perfectly logical. If you have no doubt of your premises or your power and want a certain result with all your heart you naturally express your wishes in law and sweep away all opposition. To allow opposition by speech seems to indicate that you think the speech impotent, as when a man says that he has squared the circle, or that you do not care wholeheartedly for the result, or that you doubt either your power or your premises. But when men have realized that time has upset many fighting faiths, they may come to believe even more than they believe the very foundations of their own conduct that the ultimate good desired is better reached

4 250 U. S. 627, 628.

by free trade in ideas—that the best test of truth is the power of the thought to get itself accepted in the competition of the market, and that truth is the only ground upon which their wishes safely can be carried out. That at any rate is the theory of our Constitution. It is an experiment, as all life is an experiment. Every year if not every day we have to wager our salvation upon some prophecy based upon imperfect knowledge. While that experiment is part of our system I think that we should be eternally vigilant against attempts to check the expression of opinions that we loathe and believe to be fraught with death, unless they so imminently threaten immediate interference with the lawful and pressing purposes of the law that an immediate check is required to save the country. I wholly disagree with the argument of the Government that the First Amendment left the common law as to seditious libel in force. History seems to me against the notion. I had conceived that the United States through many years had shown its repentance for the Sedition Act of 1798, by repaying fines that it imposed. Only the emergency that makes it immediately dangerous to leave the correction of evil counsels to time warrants making any exception to the sweeping command, 'Congress shall make no law . . . abridging the freedom of speech.' Of course I am speaking only of expressions of opinion and exhortations, which were all that were uttered here, but I regret that I cannot put into more impressive words my belief that in their conviction upon this indictment the defendants were deprived of their rights under the Constitution of the United States."[5]

The *Abrams* dissent was the first of six opinions by Justices Holmes and Brandeis that carried forward the genesis of "clear and present danger." With the exception of one that was a concurring opinion, all were likewise dissents. Three, including *Abrams*, were in Espionage Act cases and three were cases that involved state criminal anarchy and syndicalism statutes. In all but one the two Justices stood together, sometimes with one and sometimes with the other as spokesman.

Justice Brandeis was the spokesman in the two Espionage Act case dissents, both leaflet cases, that followed the *Abrams* dissent. In the first of these, *Schaefer* v. *United States,* he characterized "clear and present danger" as a rule of reason which, if correctly applied, would preserve freedom of speech "both from suppression

[5] 250 U. S. 616, 630, 631. Cf. Wiener, " 'Freedom for the Thought that we Hate'; is it a Principle of the Constitution?" 37 *American Bar Association Journal* 177 (1951).

by tyrannous, well meaning majorities and from abuse by irresponsible minorities." Then he went on to make interesting observations on the function of judge and jury in the application of the rule. Whether particular words were within permissible curtailment was, according to his view, a question of degree as a consequence of which the discretion of the jury should be wide in the exercise of its judgment. But, he continued, "If the words were of such a nature and were used under such circumstances that men, judging in calmness, could not reasonably say that they created a clear and present danger that they would bring about the evil that Congress sought and had a right to prevent, then it is the duty of the trial judge to withdraw the case from the consideration of the jury; if he fails to do so, it is the duty of the appellate court to correct the error."[6]

In the other Espionage Act case, *Pierce* v. *United States,* Justice Brandeis reasoned as to part of the indictment that a verdict should have been directed for the defendants not only for lack of proof of an attempt willfully to "cause insubordination, disloyalty, mutiny, or refusal of duty, in the military or naval forces" within the terms of the act, but also because the leaflet itself and the circumstances under which it was distributed were not such "as to create a clear and present danger of causing either insubordination, disloyalty, mutiny or refusal of duty in the military or naval forces." At best, the leaflet objected to, which was distributed to civilians rather than to military or naval forces, was said to contain lurid and perhaps exaggerated pictures of the horrors of war. . . .

Justice Brandeis completed the Holmes-Brandeis presentation of "clear and present danger" in the concurring opinion he wrote in the *Whitney* case. He agreed with the majority that the rights of speech and assembly are not absolute although they are fundamental, but he differed with this majority on the test to be applied to determine when a restriction should be applied to protect the state from destruction, or from political, economic or moral injury. He argued for "clear and present danger" even in the presence of a legislative pronouncement that a danger exists which calls for protective measures. To him, even though constitutional on its face, a statute must be open to challenge to determine whether the facts to which it is applied meet the test of "clear and present danger." He argued that such a statute and such a legislative pronouncement constitute but rebuttable presumptions.

[6] 251 U. S. 483 (1920).

One wonders that Holmes would go so far as to agree with this, especially in view of the extent of his belief of the right of the legislature to experiment, but agree he did.

As Justice Brandeis further elaborated on "clear and present danger" he expounded on the beliefs that he claimed motivated the adoption of the prohibitions against abridgment of speech and press. He described these as beliefs that "the final end of the State was to make men free to develop their faculties; and that in its government the deliberative forces should prevail over the arbitrary." He further characterized these as beliefs "that freedom to think as you will and to speak as you will are means indispensable to the discovery and spread of political truth; that without free speech and assembly discussion would be futile; that with them, discussion affords ordinarily adequate protection against the dissemination of noxious doctrine." Law and order, he added, could not be assured by fear and repression, but rather by free discussion of supposed grievances and proposed remedies. As he saw it, more than fear of serious injury alone is necessary to justify suppression of free speech and assembly. There must exist a contemplated evil which is so imminent that there is no opportunity for full and free discussion; there must be present a danger of such a character that the remedy of education by more speech cannot be relied on to avert the evil.

WALTER BERNS

A Critical View of the Danger Test

Of the many critics of the clear and present danger doctrine, Walter Berns, professor of government at Cornell University, is perhaps the most caustic. In this selection, he chides the liberals for their "clear and present danger cult . . . with Holmes the figure of adulation." Since Schenck, Gitlow, Abrams, Whitney, and Dennis and his communist colleagues all went to

From Walter Berns, *Freedom, Virtue, and the First Amendment* (1957), pp. 49–57. Reprinted by permission of Louisiana State University Press.

> *jail either with the doctrine or in spite of it, he wonders why the advocates of free speech should be so enamored of the danger doctrine.*

THE STORY OF THE MOST FAMOUS of the guiding principles in free speech cases, the clear and present danger test, is a tale told many times. Holmes's enunciation of it in the Schenck case has become almost as famous as his defense of it in his Abrams dissent, and the two of them together have almost attained that degree of fame for which documents are placed under glass and sealed in helium. A kind of clear-and-present-danger cult has grown up, with Holmes the figure of adulation. It was in the Schenck case, decided on March 3, 1919, that Holmes fired the shot still heard throughout the libertarian world: "The question in every case is whether the words used are used in such circumstances and are of such a nature as to create a clear and present danger that they will bring about the substantive evils that Congress has a right to prevent." One week later he sent Socialist Eugene Debs and German newspaper editor Jacob Frohwerk to jail without so much as a passing reference to the danger test, and this despite the fact that Schenck, Debs, and Frohwerk were indicted under the same law and that the cases were so similar that, to quote Holmes himself, "so far as the language of the articles goes there is not much to choose between expressions to be found in them [Frohwerk's newspapers] and those before us in *Schenck* v. *United States*." Yet, his opinions upholding the convictions of Debs and Frohwerk are explained away by his admirers. Because of this and despite all that has been written about the clear and present danger test and the general, if confused, familiarity concerning its place in constitutional law, there remains need for still another analysis, emphasizing those elements of it which bear directly on this study.

The first thing to be remembered is that Schenck was sent to jail with it. The second is that Abrams and Gitlow, with Holmes dissenting in ringing clear and present danger language, were jailed despite it. The third is that Dennis and his Communist friends were sent to jail with it. But the clear and present danger test used in the beginning was not the test used to send Dennis to prison in 1951. The transformation was not fortuitous and will be considered in its place; the point to be stressed here is that they all went to prison. Yet to listen to the praise heaped on this test by people working for free speech, one would think that it had taken its place alongside the writ of *habeas corpus* as a means of restoring freedom. It would be interesting, but perhaps not worth the effort, to count the number of defendants who have been "sprung" with this test. Professor Chafee wrote recently:

Holmes' inestimable service to free speech consisted in his getting a unanimous Supreme Court [in the Schenck case] to accept his test of guilt, which placed a great area of discussion beyond the reach of the government. . . . Over eight years would go by before a majority of the Court would apply Holmes' test so as to let anyone out of prison. Still, the "clear and present danger" test did eventually reverse many convictions, and no doubt it staved off many prosecutions which would otherwise have taken place both in peace and during the Second World War.[1]

His reference is to *Fiske* v. *Kansas,* a case coming to the Court eight years after the Schenck case; but there is not a suggestion of the clear and present danger test in the Court's opinion. Fiske had been convicted of violating a state syndicalism act, but Justice Sanford said for the unanimous Court: "Thus applied the Act is an arbitrary and unreasonable exercise of the police power of the State, unwarrantably infringing the liberty of the defendant in violation of the due process clause of the Fourteenth Amendment." In another place Professor Chafee warns the reader not to overlook the great importance of the Fiske decision simply because it contained no "ringing phrases and does not even use the words, 'freedom of speech and assembly.' " The real significance of the case lies in the fact that "Fiske was heard and released because he was deprived of liberty of speech under a statute which, though constitutional in itself, had been construed to punish utterances which were now held to be immune under the United States Constitution. In *Fiske* v. *Kansas* the Supreme Court for the first time made freedom of speech mean something."[2] And it did so without using the clear and present danger test.

Another writer states, "Although Justice Holmes initiated the rule with the support of a unanimous Court, it was not until 1937

---

[1] "Thirty-Five Years with Freedom of Speech," pamphlet published by the Roger N. Baldwin Civil Liberties Foundation (May, 1952), 8.

[2] Chafee, *Free Speech,* 352.

that a majority of that body applied it favorably."[3] The reference here is to *Herndon* v. *Lowry* and since he has taken the trouble to list every case in which the doctrine was cited, his view of the facts must be given some weight. It is the opinion of the present writer that the Supreme Court, at least, has overturned only one conviction on the basis of the clear and present danger doctrine— when that doctrine has been applied to a situation *for which it was designed.* To support this statement, it will not be argued that a doctrine must remain static, incapable of expansion, but that the expansion must occur only within carefully defined limits in order to avoid distortion. The confusion surrounding the meaning of the clear and present danger test by the time of the Dennis case is evidence of what happened to "the most just and workable standard yet evolved," when it was pushed, like a drayhorse onto a race track, into service for which it was not equipped.

By analyzing each case in which it has been cited, in either the majority or a dissenting opinion, according to the claim competing with the claim to freedom of speech, an interesting pattern is discovered. The competing claim in the Schenck case, the case that gave birth to the doctrine, was the national security of the United States. Schenck's conviction was affirmed; his socialist antiwar pamphlets were held to constitute a clear and present danger of bringing about an evil that Congress had a right to prevent: the obstruction of the recruitment of the armed forces. The competing claim in the Abrams case was the same national security; Abrams' conviction was affirmed, though Holmes and Brandeis argued that his leaflets, the "puny anonymities," did not constitute a clear and present danger. The same is true in *Gitlow* v. *New York, Schaefer* v. *United States, Pierce* v. *United States, Korematsu* v. *United States, American Communication Ass.* v. *Douds, Dennis* v. *United States,* and in the two state cases of *Gilbert* v. *Minnesota,* and *Whitney* v. *California.* And this just about exhausts the list of cases in which the clear and present danger test was cited and did not succeed in protecting speech.

The question arises, how many times did speech triumph over this claim to national security as a result of the application of the clear and present danger test? There are four possibilities: *Herndon* v. *Lowry, Schneiderman* v. *United States, Hartzel* v. *United States,* and *Taylor* v. *Mississippi.* In the first of these, *Herndon* v. *Lowry,*

---

[3] Phillip Leonard Sirotkin, "The Evolution of the Clear and Present Danger Doctrine" (Unpublished master's thesis, Department of Political Science, University of Chicago, 1947), 2.

the facts indicate that though Herndon was a Communist, the state of Georgia was not really concerned with the national security. He was convicted under a pre-Civil War statute aimed at those who would attempt to incite slaves to insurrection. A divided Court reversed his conviction. Justice Roberts said: "And, where a statute is so vague and uncertain as to make criminal an utterance or an act which may be innocently said or done with no intent to induce resort to violence or on the other hand may be said or done with a purpose violently to subvert government, a conviction under such a law cannot be sustained." He also referred to freedom of speech: "The power of a state to abridge freedom of speech and of association is the exception rather than the rule and the penalizing even of utterances of a defined character must find its justification in a reasonable apprehension of danger to organized government." But not even Professor Chafee contends that the Court relied on the clear and present danger test to reverse this conviction. Herndon was freed, but not with the danger test.

Schneiderman was a Communist and a naturalized citizen. The government tried to revoke his citizenship on the basis of his failure to admit membership in the Communist Party at the time he was naturalized; it also claimed that no Communist Party member could honestly swear to support the Constitution of the United States. This, then, is not technically a speech case, but raises questions more properly considered under the rubric of freedom of association. The minority of four, speaking through Chief Justice Stone, denied that speech was involved, and seemed willing to consider it an association case in which the intentions of the Communist Party would have been relevant. The majority had to indulge in some prestidigitation to introduce the speech issue, but even then did not forbid his denaturalization on the basis of freedom of speech and the clear and present danger test. ". . . this is a denaturalization proceeding in which, if the Government is entitled to attack a finding of attachment as we have assumed, the burden rests upon it to prove the alleged lack of attachment by 'clear, unequivocal and convincing' evidence. That burden has not been carried. The Government has not proved that petitioner's beliefs on the subject of force and violence were such that he was not attached to the Constitution in 1927." It was not the danger test that rescued Schneiderman.

Hartzel was convicted under the Espionage Act of 1917, as amended, the same statute under which Schenck was sent to jail.

Justice Murphy, who wrote the opinion, insisted that the government prove "beyond a reasonable doubt" that the petitioner had a "specific intent or evil purpose" in distributing his literature and that his activities "will bring about the substantive evils which Congress has a right to prevent." The government failed to establish evil intent, which made a detailed consideration of the clear and present danger aspects of Hartzel's activities unnecessary. This distinction between intent and clear and present danger is a valid one on the basis of the Schenck case, for Holmes too had kept them separate in his opinion. Thus, this conviction was reversed primarily because of the government's failure to prove evil intent, a view which, to say nothing more, the minority did not share.

This brings us to *Taylor* v. *Mississippi*. With a rare unanimity in this sort of case, the Court reversed the conviction of a Jehovah's Witness who had run afoul of a war-time state sedition law by publicly urging people not to support the war or salute the flag. The Court said:

The statute as construed in these cases makes it a criminal offense to communicate to others views and opinions respecting governmental policies, and prophecies concerning the future of our own and other nations. As applied to the appellants it punishes them although what they communicated is not claimed or shown to have been done with an evil or sinister purpose, to have advocated or incited subversive action against the nation or state, or to have threatened any clear and present danger to our institutions or our Government. What these appellants communicated were their beliefs and opinions concerning domestic measures and trends in national and world affairs.

Under our decision criminal sanctions cannot be imposed for such communication.[4]

Of these four cases, then, only one, the last, can illustrate the use of the clear and present danger doctrine to cause the triumph of free speech over national security, and it could be argued that Taylor and his fellow defendants were freed under the long-established common law rule that there must be proof of intent. Thus, in this area, the area in which the rule was first enunciated, the clear and present danger test has been of assistance only to a Jehovah's Witness—not to a Socialist like Debs or a Communist like Gitlow or Dennis, or to anyone else whose opinions are both hated *and* feared. In every other case in which it played a part, the con-

[4] U.S. 583, 589–590 (1943).

viction of the defendant was upheld. The clear and present danger test actually becomes a rationale for avoiding the impossible prohibitions of the First Amendment and for convicting persons for speech that the government has forbidden. Professor Chafee may prefer to look upon the test as "placing a great area of discussion beyond the reach of the government," but it is closer to the facts to regard the test as placing a great area of discussion *within* the reach of the government.

The purpose of the above analysis will now be made clearer. If, in that area where speech conflicts with the security of the nation, the clear and present danger test has proved a poor defense for the accused speakers, how has the test attained its fame? The answer is evident as soon as we shift our attention to those cases where speech has come in conflict with claims other than national security. The quickest glance at the list of these reveals what might appear to be an insignificant difference from the first list, but it actually represents a vital difference: a frequent party to the litigation in the first category does not appear in the second, namely, the United States. With but rare exceptions it is no longer the United States versus Schenck, Abrams, Pierce, Schaefer, Korematsu, and so forth. Now the litigants are usually private persons versus states or municipalities: *Cantwell* v. *Connecticut, Pennekamp* v. *Florida,* and *Terminiello* v. *Chicago.* The problems in these cases are not only different from national security cases, but the convictions here were reversed. Until quite recently, whenever freedom of speech has vied with claims other than national security it has emerged triumphant. This has been accomplished by means of the clear and present danger test and its extension, the preferred position doctrine. These cases have been hailed as great victories for freedom.

Used in cases as remote from the situation in the Schenck case as those involving labor picketing and contempt of court, it is no wonder that the clear and present danger test was almost unrecognizable by the time the Court called upon it to convict Dennis. But despite Professor Fellman's sardonic remark, "Whether the clear and present danger doctrine will survive much longer under the crushing weight of the Chief Justice's loving devotion remains to be seen,"[5] it was not Vinson's fault that the test was not the chaste, unsullied debutante of 1919; it had spent over thirty years in the streets. Judge Learned Hand's explication of these years in

[5] "Constitutional Law in 1950–1951," *American Political Science Review,* XLVI (March, 1952), 162.

his opinion for the Circuit Court of Appeals, showing the twists and turns in the test's development, ought to be sufficient to exonerate the late Chief Justice from the charge that he had distorted the meaning of a simple, clearly understood and applied judicial principle. Had there been a thirty-year hiatus between the Pierce case and the Dennis case, that is, had the test not been misapplied, Vinson might have dealt as neatly with Dennis as Holmes had with Schenck, perhaps repeating the clear and present danger slogan and winning a niche in the liberals' hall of fame. But there was no hiatus; Vinson had to deal with the difficult problem of *stare decisis* and the Court's decisions in cases like *Cantwell* v. *Connecticut, Thornhill* v. *Alabama,* and *Thomas* v. *Collins.* He ought to have been spared this onerous duty; and despite statements of doubtful validity, such as that the prevention of the forceful overthrow of the government "is the ultimate value of any society . . . ," his opinion does not deserve *all* the scorn heaped upon it by Professor Fellman and others. The danger test is not a panacea.

THE PREFERRED POSITION DOCTRINE

MR. JUSTICE WILEY RUTLEDGE

A Preference for First Amendment Freedoms

Wiley B. Rutledge had served as Dean of the State University of Iowa Law School and as a judge on a U.S. Court of Appeals prior to his appointment by President Franklin Roosevelt in 1943 to the Supreme Court. The opinion written by Justice Rutledge in Thomas v. Collins *(1944), edited below, is noted for*

Justice Wiley B. Rutledge speaking for the majority in *Thomas v. Collins,* 323 U. S. 516 (1945). Case citations omitted.

> *its statement of the preferred-position doctrine and for the link-*
> *age it makes between this doctrine and the clear-and-present-*
> *danger test. Basic to the preferred position is the view that First*
> *Amendment freedoms are essential to the operation of a demo-*
> *cratic society. Therefore, freedom of speech, freedom of press,*
> *freedom to assemble and to petition against grievances are to*
> *be preferred when faced with a challenge of a competing legal*
> *claim. This preference can be overturned only by a showing of*
> *a clear and present danger to a substantial interest that gov-*
> *ernment has a right to protect. In* Thomas v. Collins, *the*
> *legislature of Texas had enacted a law requiring all persons*
> *soliciting members for labor unions to register with the sec-*
> *retary of state. Mr. Thomas, President of the U.A.W. and*
> *Vice-President of the C.I.O., deliberately challenged this act*
> *by soliciting members for a union without observing the regis-*
> *tration provisions. From adverse decisions at the state level,*
> *Mr. Thomas appealed to the Supreme Court on grounds that*
> *his right to freedom of speech had been infringed. The Court*
> *sustained the free speech claim and declared the Texas law*
> *unconstitutional.*

THE CASE CONFRONTS US AGAIN with the duty our system places on this Court to say where the individual's freedom ends and the State's power begins. Choice on that border, now as always deli- cate, is perhaps more so where the usual presumption supporting legislation is balanced by the preferred place given in our scheme to the great, the indispensable democratic freedoms secured by the First Amendment. . . . That priority gives these liberties a sanctity and a sanction not permitting dubious intrusions. And it is the character of the right, not of the limitation, which determines what standard governs the choice. . . .

For these reasons any attempt to restrict those liberties must be justified by clear public interest, threatened not doubtfully or re- motely, but by clear and present danger. The rational connection between the remedy provided and the evil to be curbed, which in other contexts might support legislation against attack on due pro- cess grounds, will not suffice. These rights rest on firmer founda- tion. Accordingly, whatever occasion would restrain orderly discus- sion and persuasion, at appropriate time and place, must have clear support in public danger, actual or impending. Only the gravest abuses, endangering paramount interests, give occasion for permissible limitation. It is therefore in our tradition to allow the widest room for discussion, the narrowest range for its restriction, particularly when this right is exercised in conjunction with peaceable assembly. It was not by accident or coincidence that the rights to freedom in speech and press were coupled in a single guaranty with the rights of the people peaceably to assemble and to petition for redress of grievances. All these, though not identical, are inseparable. They are cognate rights, . . . and therefore are united in the First Article's assurance. . . .

This conjunction of liberties is not peculiar to religious activity and institutions alone. The First Amendment gives freedom of mind the same security as freedom of conscience. . . . Great secular causes, with small ones, are guarded. The grievances for redress of which the right of petition was insured, and with it the right of assembly, are not solely religious or political ones. And the rights of free speech and a free press are not confined to any field of human interest.

The idea is not sound therefore that the First Amendment's safeguards are wholly inapplicable to business or economic activity. And it does not resolve where the line shall be drawn in a particular case merely to urge, as Texas does, that an organization for which the rights of free speech and free assembly are claimed is one "engaged in business activities" or that the individual who leads it in exercising these rights receives compensation for doing so. Nor, on the other hand, is the answer given, whether what is done is an exercise of those rights and the restriction a forbidden impairment, by ignoring the organization's economic function, because those interests of workingmen are involved or because they have the general liberties of the citizen, as appellant would do.

These comparisons are at once too simple, too general, and too inaccurate to be determinative. Where the line shall be placed in a particular application rests, not on such generalities, but on the concrete clash of particular interests and the community's relative evaluation both of them and of how the one will be affected by the specific restriction, the other by its absence. That judgment in the first instance is for the legislative body. But in our system where the line can constitutionally be placed presents a question this Court cannot escape answering independently, whatever the legislative judgment, in the light of our constitutional tradition. . . . And the answer, under that tradition, can be affirmative, to support an intrusion upon this domain, only if grave and impending public danger requires this.

That the State has power to regulate labor unions with a view to protecting the public interest is, as the Texas court said, hardly to be doubted. They cannot claim special immunity from regulation. Such regulation however, whether aimed at fraud or other abuses, must not trespass upon the domains set apart for free speech and free assembly. This Court has recognized that "in the circumstances of our times the dissemination of information concerning the facts of a labor dispute must be regarded as within that area of free discussion that is guaranteed by the Constitution. . . . Free discussion concerning the conditions in industry and the causes of labor disputes appears to us indispensable to the effective and intelligent use of the processes of popular government to shape the destiny of modern industrial society." . . . The right thus to discuss, and inform people concerning, the advantages and disadvantages of unions and joining them is protected not only as part of free speech, but as part of free assembly. . . . The Texas court, in its disposition of the cause, did not give sufficient weight to this consideration, more particularly by its failure to take account of the blanketing effect of the prohibition's present application upon public discussion and also of the bearing of the clear and present danger test in these circumstances.

The restraint is not small when it is considered what was restrained. The right is a national right, federally guaranteed. There is some modicum of freedom of thought, speech and assembly which all citizens of the Republic may exercise throughout its length and breadth, which no State, nor all together, nor the Nation itself, can prohibit, restrain or impede. If the restraint were smaller than it is, it is from petty tyrannies that large ones take root and grow. This fact can be no more plain than when they are imposed on the most basic rights of all. Seedlings planted in that soil grow great and, growing, break down the foundations of liberty. . . .

The judgment is reversed.

MR. JUSTICE FELIX FRANKFURTER

The Preferred Position: "A Mischievous Phrase"

Felix Frankfurter was a professor of law at Harvard Law School and an Assistant U.S. Attorney prior to being appointed to the Supreme Court by Franklin Roosevelt in 1939. He served on the Court until 1962. In a concurring opinion in Kovacs v. Cooper *(1949), reprinted below, Justice Frankfurter set forth his objections to the preferred-position doctrine as an approach to the interpretation of the First Amendment.*

MY BROTHER REED SPEAKS of "the preferred position of freedom of speech.". . . . This is a phrase that has uncritically crept into some recent opinions of this Court. I deem it a mischievous phrase, if it carries the thought, which it may subtly imply, that any law touching communication is infected with presumptive invalidity. It is not the first time in the history of constitutional adjudication that such a doctrinaire attitude has disregarded the admonition most to be observed in exercising the Court's reviewing power over legislation, "that it is *a constitution* we are expounding.". . . . I say the phrase is mischievous because it radiates a constitutional doctrine without avowing it. . . .

Behind the notion sought to be expressed by the formula as to "the preferred position of freedom of speech" lies a relevant consideration in determining whether an enactment relating to the liberties protected by the Due Process Clause of the Fourteenth Amendment is violative of it. In law also, doctrine is illuminated by history. The ideas now governing the constitutional protection of freedom of speech derive essentially from the opinions of Mr. Justice Holmes.

The philosophy of his opinions on that subject arose from a deep awareness of the extent to which sociological conclusions are con-

Justice Felix Frankfurter speaking in *Kovacs v. Cooper*, 336 U. S. 77 (1949). Case citations omitted.

ditioned by time and circumstance. Because of this awareness Mr. Justice Holmes seldom felt justified in opposing his own opinion to economic views which the legislature embodied in law. But since he also realized that the progress of civilization is to a considerable extent the displacement of error which once held sway as official truth by beliefs which in turn have yielded to other beliefs, for him the right to search for truth was of a different order than some transient economic dogma. And without freedom of expression, thought becomes checked and atrophied. Therefore, in considering what interests are so fundamental as to be enshrined in the Due Process Clause, those liberties of the individual which history has attested as the indispensable conditions of an open as against a closed society come to this Court with a momentum for respect lacking when appeal is made to liberties which derive merely from shifting economic arrangements. Accordingly, Mr. Justice Holmes was far more ready to find legislative invasion where free inquiry was involved than in the debatable area of economics. See my Mr. Justice Holmes and the Supreme Court, 58 et seq.

The objection to summarizing this line of thought by the phrase "the preferred position of freedom of speech" is that it expresses a complicated process of constitutional adjudication by a deceptive formula. And it was Mr. Justice Holmes who admonished us that "To rest upon a formula is a slumber that, prolonged, means death.". . . Such a formula makes for mechanical jurisprudence.

Some of the arguments made in this case strikingly illustrate how easy it is to fall into the ways of mechanical jurisprudence through the use of oversimplified formulas. It is argued that the Constitution protects freedom of speech: freedom of speech means the right to communicate, whatever the physical means for so doing; sound trucks are one form of communication; *ergo* that form is entitled to the same protection as any other means of communication, whether by tongue or pen. Such sterile argumentation treats society as though it consisted of bloodless categories. . . .

ROBERT B. McKAY

"The Preference for Freedom": A Rebuttal to Frankfurter

Robert B. McKay is a professor of Law and the Associate Dean at New York University School of Law. Here, he supports the preference for First Amendment freedoms and castigates Justice Frankfurter.

THE CENTRAL, THE INESCAPABLE PROPOSITION to which this study is directed is the notion that the freedom of expression is so vital in its relationship to the objectives of the Constitution that inevitably it must stand in a preferred position. In looking toward the fulfillment of that objective, there are a variety of devices, to be employed separately or in combination, which enable the courts to express the constitutionally mandated preference for freedom of speech and thought. Among these are the clear and present danger test; narrowing of the presumption of constitutionality; strict construction of statutes to avoid limitation of first amendment freedoms; the prohibitions against prior restraint and subsequent punishment; relaxation of the requirement of standing to sue where first amendment issues are involved; and generally higher standards of procedural due process where these freedoms are in jeopardy. Not one, but the sum total of these—and more—make up the preferred position concept. They embody the principled response of a judiciary alert to its highest duty—that of preserving and fostering the republic in the only way it can be made to survive—through assiduous striving after the "blessings of liberty."

It is often suggested that the preferred position originated in 1938 in Justice Stone's now-celebrated footnote in the *Carolene* case. Except for the frequency of reiteration of this misconception, refutation would scarcely be necessary. Now, however, a word may

From Robert B. McKay, "The Preference for Freedom," *New York University Law Review* (November, 1959), Vol. 34, pp. 1184–1185, 1189–1193. Reprinted by permission of the *New York University Law Review* and of the author.

be appropriate. In the first place, he did not use the words pre-ferred position in that footnote, but spoke only of the narrowing of the presumption of constitutionality as to statutes impinging on rights protected by the Bill of Rights. When, four years later, Chief Justice Stone first spoke of the preferred position, there is no indi-cation that he intended anything but the widest scope for the phrase. Certainly he did not tie the words to the earlier footnote in the *Carolene* case by citation of that case or even by reference to pre-sumptions of constitutionality of legislation. Rather, he spoke in sweeping terms:

> The First Amendment is not confined to safeguarding freedom of speech and freedom of religion against discriminatory attempts to wipe them out. On the contrary, the Constitution, by virtue of the First and Fourteenth Amendments, has put those freedoms in a preferred position.[1]

In short, Chief Justice Stone should be credited with the expression, but he of course did not claim authorship of the idea that lies be-hind that neatly capsulized reminder of the proper significance of the first amendment freedoms.

Where, then, are the proper beginnings? The American origins arise out of the discussion and correspondence, principally between Jefferson and Madison, that led to the proposing and adoption of the first amendment. Behind that decision to have an explicit pro-hibition upon governmental interference with speech and thought was the consciousness of centuries of less than freedom in England and the Colonies. Justice Black has stated forcefully this awareness:

> No purpose in ratifying the Bill of Rights was clearer than that of securing for the people of the United States much greater freedom of religion, expression, assembly, and petition than the people of Great Britain had ever enjoyed.[2]

That these considerations were indeed uppermost in the mind of Madison, the proposer of the first amendment, has been fully docu-mented by Professor Cahn. It is especially significant to observe that Madison demonstrated a willingness to grade the rights within the Bill of Rights, and that in his judgment "the freedoms embodied in the First Amendment must always secure paramountcy." Thus, it is

---

[1] Jones v. Opelika, 316 U.S. 584, 608 (1942) (dissenting opinion).
[2] Bridges v. California, 314 U.S. 252, 265 (1941).

clear that the two concepts which are central to the preferred position theory—primacy of the rights of mind and conscience, and the need for choice even within the Bill of Rights—can both be traced unmistakably to the period before 1791 when the first amendment was ratified. . . .

All Justices who have sat on the United States Supreme Court since 1919, and who have had occasion to express themselves on the first amendment, have accorded a special significance to its command. The fact to be particularly noted is that this preference for the first or grading, as it has been called, has not been indulged in exclusively by the past and present libertarians on the Court. Even when the Court held that a claimed right did not come within first amendment protection, it has been the not-infrequent custom to preface the denial with a reminder of the special favoritism with which the first amendment should be regarded. Lest this seem anomalous it should be remembered that the right is not absolute, and in many instances the questions for decision are close and difficult. A sample of some of the opinions over the intervening years demonstrates the uniform acknowledgment that the first amendment does stand apart—and above. . . .

At this point it is necessary only to note that every member of the Court since 1919 has concurred in one on many of the collected expressions of preference for the first amendment. The issue, if issue there ever was, would no longer seem to be an open one. The first amendment *does* stand in a preferred position.

One Justice, and apparently only one, has taken some pains to deny that the first amendment is to be preferred; but one can find even in his opinions considerable indication of the favored place conferred upon the freedoms of speech and thought. The reference of course is to Justice Frankfurter who has at least four times denied that he accords to the first amendment a preferred position.

There is an aura of unreality about the debate over whether the first amendment has or should have a preferred position. Had the validity of the preferred position doctrine not been contested by so able a scholar and judge as Justice Frankfurter, it would seem the purest show of pedantry to review the origins and standing of the concept. Perhaps the difficulty has arisen from the fact that the preferred position concept does no more than state a mood; its admonitory quality recalls to mind the simple but majestic fact that here is a society in which the important freedoms count for something. Even if other values, almost equally precious, must on occasion be sacrificed, the price is not too great to preserve unblemished the safeguards of liberty.

The difficulty in this unreal dispute between disputants who do not disagree, then, has perhaps been a failure to accept the full constitutional implications of the preference for freedom. To attempt to reduce the core principle of democracy to a formula, however malleable, is to sacrifice its essential worth. To fragmentize the grand design of the idea of freedom is inevitably to reduce the sum of the parts to something less than the whole. But the question has been raised, and it is therefore important to accept and answer the challenge.

It has already been shown that the first amendment has been accorded a preferred position in this larger sense at least since 1791. Thus, it is clearly inaccurate to speak of the preferred position concept as having been derived from Justice Stone's magnificently ambiguous footnote in the *Carolene* case. It is equally incorrect to credit the inception of the concept, as does Justice Frankfurter, to *Herndon v. Lowry.* If one is reluctant to trace origins before 1791, or even back to that year as a starting point, it appears essential to recognize at least that the original formulation of the clear and present danger test by Justice Holmes in *Schenck v. United States* was a recognition that when first amendment values are involved, the otherwise permissible prohibitions which government might impose are to be examined in a different context and measured by a more critical standard. This, then, is the essence of the preferred position—the exercise of judgment to protect first amendment freedoms in a variety of ways.

It remains, then, only to note why it is that Justice Frankfurter dissents from what seems otherwise to be harmonious agreement. Four observations come to mind.

First. Justice Frankfurter has objected several times to the expression preferred position, which he regards as a "mischievous phrase." His principal argument appears in a concurring opinion in *Kovacs v. Cooper,* where it becomes clear that whatever his difference with the majority may be in terms of semantics, it scarcely amounts to a difference in substance. The ostensible disagreement is with "the thought, which it may subtly imply, that any law touching communication is infected with presumptive invalidity." There are two difficulties with this argument. In the first place, neither the cases he cites nor the somewhat more extended list included in the appendix to this study justify his conclusion that the doctrine has ever been so regarded. Rather, as Justice Stone remarked in the *Carolene* footnote, "there may be narrower scope for the presumption of constitutionality when legislation appears on its face to be within a specific prohibition of the Constitution, such as those of the first ten amendments. . . ."[3] That is, legislation claimed to impinge on rights of free speech and thought should be inspected more critically by the judiciary than where exclusively economic rights are at issue. But this is emphatically not to say that those who agree that the first amendment is to be preferred start with a presumption that controlling legislation is unconstitutional where it touches free speech. Thus, Justice Reed, writing for the majority in *Kovacs v. Cooper*, said that "the preferred position of freedom of speech in a society that cherishes liberty for all does not require legislators to be insensible to claims by citizens to comfort and convenience."

The second and more important difficulty with his argument is that it too narrowly conceives the concept of preferred position. The whole question as to the presumption of constitutionality of legislation is simply a part—and not the most important part—of what should properly be regarded as the reach of the preferred position. That concept represents a whole manner of approaching freedom of speech and thought. To miss this is to miss the point altogether.

Second. If Justice Frankfurter intends to reject the primacy of the first amendment he stands alone. But that does not seem to be a correct statement of his position. For he has made in *Kovacs v. Cooper* a statement of credo which is one of the most eloquent testimonials to the vitality of the preferred position concept:

[W]ithout freedom of expression, thought becomes checked and atrophied. Therefore, in considering what interests are so fundamental as to be enshrined in the Due Process Clause, those liberties of the individual which history has attested as the indispensable conditions of an open as against a closed society come to this Court with a momentum for respect lacking when appeal is made to liberties which derive merely from shifting economic arrangements.

Justice Rutledge, in reference to these words, drily remarked that:

[3] United States v. Carolene Prods. Co., 304 U.S. 144, 152 n.4 (1938).

I think my brother Frankfurter demonstrates the conclusion opposite to that which he draws, namely, that the First Amendment guaranties of the freedoms of speech, press, assembly, and religion occupy preferred position not only in the Bill of Rights but also in the repeated decision of this Court.

Third. As long as he has been on the Court, Justice Frankfurter has insisted on the grading of rights. He clearly differentiates among the provisions of the Bill of Rights, believing that not all its guarantees are "of the very essence of a scheme of ordered liberty," and that those which do not so measure up are not deserving of incorporation into the fourteenth amendment as limitations upon the states. As already indicated, he agrees that the first amendment comes within the charmed circle, but he would exclude others. Is not this an expression of preference?

Fourth. Not only has Justice Frankfurter thus demonstrated his willingness to grade rights on the basis of considerations not explicitly stated in the Constitution—and thus his willingness to have the Court sit in judgment over legislative findings based on various and unspecified judicial criteria—but he has also proved willing to grade rights even *within* the first amendment. His preference for freedom of religion is unmistakable. What, then, remains of his reluctance to use the term preferred position? Is it simply a refusal to concede that he does not defer to legislative findings in these cases as in others, or does it conceal the application of idiosyncratic standards not ascertainable in advance?

PAUL G. KAUPER

The Balance-of-Interest Approach

How do we decide what speech is protected and what should be banned? Paul G. Kauper, professor of law at the University of Michigan Law School, provides an explanation of the balance-of-interest approach to this problem. According to Professor Kauper, this approach contains the best features of American jurisprudence: it is pragmatic and empirical in the case method of judicial determination. As applied to the problem of American communists, the balance-of-interest approach will take into account all the values that must be weighed. On the one hand, there is our interest in the right to dissent, to advocate change, to join organizations with like purposes, while on the other hand, Congress and the majority of citizens have an interest in maintaining constitutional order.

IN DEFENSE OF THE BALANCE-OF-INTEREST APPROACH subscribed to by a present majority of the Court, it is accurate to say that it represents the dominant philosophy of constitutional interpretation of the modern era. If there is anything that distinguishes American constitutional interpretation, it is the pragmatic process as distinguished from formal conceptualism or a verbalism that turns on the words used within the four corners of the instrument. This has been the whole history of the Due Process Clause of the Fourteenth Amendment. Indeed, it may be said that the interpretation of the Due Process Clause affords less protection to the substantive liberties than the balance-of-interest technique if due process is inter-

Reprinted from *Civil Liberties and the Constitution* (1962), pp. 117–126, by Paul G. Kauper, by permission of the University of Michigan Press. Copyright © by The University of Michigan, 1962. All rights reserved.

preted by reference to Justice Holmes' reasonable man. But at least it is clear that over the long run due process has meant an empiric interpretation by the Court based on the facts of the problem before the Court and its weighing of competing interests. This is evident also in other fields of constitutional interpretation and notably in regard to the problems of federalism as they relate to the distribution of powers between the federal government and the states. The Court has abandoned all pretense of defining federal powers in conceptual terms that are designed to place limits on the federal government. The old idea that commerce meant certain things and that Congress could not legislate beyond the reach of the powers so designed has been abandoned by the Court. A determination by Congress that certain legislation is necessary and proper in order to carry out certain functions is likely to be sustained by the Court as long as some rational consideration supports the Congressional determination, as against the claim that the subject matter belongs to the reserved powers of the states. The pragmatic approach by the Court is evidenced particularly by the cases involving the question of state power to tax and to regulate commerce. The *Southern Pacific* case gives us an excellent illustration of the judicial balancing of national and local interests where the question was raised whether local legislation interfering with freedom of interstate transportation was valid.

Consider also the interpretation of the provision of the Fifth Amendment that private property shall not be taken for public use without just compensation. Although this appears absolute, still critical questions of construction arise and within the limits of this language a balancing process takes place. For instance, the question is raised whether zoning regulation amounts to a taking of property. The Court has said this is not a taking, although it is evident that zoning does in fact impair property interests and does in fact amount to a taking in the public interest of the uses prohibited to the owner. The Court has said, however, that this is a reasonable exercise of the police power, and there is no longer any real quarrel over the result. What the Court is doing here is balancing interests in determining what the appropriate public interests are that can be served by police legislation in limiting private property rights and what community interests can be advanced at the expense of private property only by exercise of the condemnation power.

In stating the opinion that the so-called absolute interpretation of the First Amendment is not absolute and that within the range of the literal interpretation there is still wide room for judicial maneuvering which requires an evaluation of competing interests, I do not mean to depreciate an interpretation which seeks to lend pre-eminence to the First Amendment freedoms and which employs the absolute interpretation as a vehicle for achieving this result. On the other hand, I suggest that the balance-of-interest approach is one that finds warrant in the main stream of American constitutional interpretation. If the balance-of-interest technique is to be used, however, it must be done in a way that does justice to constitutional values.

With specific reference to the First Amendment freedoms, the balance-of-interest technique approach affords a useful approach, first of all, in that the Court may more carefully discriminate as to the various facets of freedom there protected. One weakness of the absolute interpretation of the First Amendment and of the general statement that First Amendment freedoms are preferred freedoms is that it tends to ignore the consideration that not all forms of expression stand on the same level in terms of their constitutional importance. Moreover, abridgment may take the form of direct or indirect abridgment, and again this distinction is relevant to the balancing of interests.

It is speech in the sphere of political activities and concerned with matters of public interest that should be the highest and the preferred speech value under the First Amendment. This is the aspect of speech that most clearly distinguishes a democratic society. This includes the freedom to dissent, to express non-conforming ideas, to advocate change, the freedom, indeed, to advocate a new type of social and economic and political structure and to join in political association with others for this purpose. The only justification for laws restricting sedition and advocacy of violent change is that under our system there is abundant opportunity for change by peaceable methods and for this reason the First Amendment freedoms assume a paramount importance in their political aspects. For this reason any approach simply in terms of reasonableness does not do justice to these freedoms as they relate to matters of public concern. The balance-of-interest approach does offer an approach which is consistent with the importance of these freedoms and at the same time is consistent with public interests that may be appropriately served by Congress and the states. The important question is in what way the Court balances these freedoms.

The question may then be raised whether the Court in its decisions dealing with Communists has used the balance-of-interest technique in a way that has undermined and devitalized the First Amendment freedoms. This hardly applies to the recent decision upholding the registration requirement of the Internal Security Act. The public interest in requiring the public identification of a party that is controlled by a foreign government and which has as its objectives the establishment by conspiratorial, revolutionary methods of a Soviet type of dictatorship is clear, and the impact on freedom of political discussion is secondary and indirect. For the same reason there can be no serious objection to the study and examination by a Congressional committee of Communist propaganda and of methods used by the Communist Party in promoting its objectives. Likewise, in view of the nature of the Communist Party, as supported by the determination of the Subversive Activities Control Board, it seems that a substantial public interest warrants an inquiry into Communist affiliation of public employers or of persons seeking admission to the bar.

More difficulty is raised by the decisions upholding the power of a Congressional committee to require a witness to disclose Communist affiliation. In conceding a power of Congress to investigate Communism, it does not necessarily follow that a committee should be allowed to force a man to disclose or deny Communist affiliation at a public hearing which can too easily be converted into a public trial aimed at exposure and without serving any substantial purpose related to the legitimate Congressional interest into the penetration of Communism into various fields of activity. Whether alternative methods are available for achieving the investigative purpose is a factor properly taken into account in any balance of interest. It cannot be seriously argued that Congress or the federal government is without adequate means to inform itself about the Communist movement unless individuals can be forced to disclose their affiliations at a public hearing. The weakness of the *Barenblatt* case in applying the balance-of-interest technique is that the Court did not adequately consider and weigh the necessity of getting the information in this particular way.

The interpretations of the Smith Act relating to the conspiracy and knowing membership clauses present difficulties, too. Admittedly, the governmental interest in protecting against use of violence in the achievement of change is a paramount interest. Too, the fact that concerted activity supports a conspiracy theory is important. But whether the balance should be struck at the point where advocacy is an incitement to future criminal conduct or, as the dissenters contend, at the point where it does in fact incite to criminal conduct, is the problem. Justice Holmes and Brandeis were not absolutists and were ready to balance interests. But in dealing with political speech they balanced speech heavily and required a showing that the speech presented a clear, present, and substantial danger of a public evil within the power of Congress to prohibit or punish. Whether in view of the nature of the Communist conspiracy a lesser test should apply is the question. In this area of speech, where the Court has before it a criminal statute aimed directly at speech, it should be the Court's function in balancing of interests to determine whether, on the record presented to the Court, the danger resulting from the speech is of sufficient weight to warrant the restriction. Certainly, the Court's careful review of the evidence in the *Yates* and *Scales* cases demonstrates that a majority of the Court are not willing to support convictions on the basis alone of participation in Communist Party activities, for some of these activities fall within the sphere of legitimate speech. But even if it is demonstrated that Communists have by their speech incited to future criminal conduct, it should remain open to judicial inquiry whether the danger presented in the case before the Court is of sufficient magnitude to warrant punishment under a criminal statute. It must be remembered that in the cases arising under the Smith Act it is not the Communist Party that is on trial but individual persons charged either with conspiring illegal advocacy or with active and purposive membership in a party guilty of such conspiracy. The question that may well be raised is whether the Court in balancing interests in the Smith Act cases has sufficiently weighed the gravity and substantiality of the danger to the national security on the facts of the case before it in determining where to strike the balance between protected and unprotected speech.

The basic issue involved in this whole area of constitutional adjudication is the question of the wise and proper use of judicial power in reconciling power and freedom. Whatever the formal doctrinal apparatus employed in dealing with the problem, the judge's own basic predisposition and his conception of the judicial power will play influential parts.

There is certainly a respectable line of authority and tradition to support the view that since the power of judicial review is an extraordinary power it should be sparingly exercised, particularly when faced with the question of Congressional authority, and that in the case of such a conflict the Court should be slow to set aside the expression of the legislative will. On the other hand, there is the view that the whole purpose of a written constitution and the institution of judicial review is to enforce restraints against the government and that a court should not be inhibited by the sense of self-restraint or in deference to the legislative determination. And certainly the extent to which the judge identifies himself with certain constitutional values and lifts them to a high point in his thinking will, in turn, govern his decision on specific issues. This dilemma and, in turn, the high degree of judicial subjectivity involved in the whole process of review create the problem which as far as I can see will always persist as long as we have judicial review of legislation. This problem becomes particularly acute when we consider the First Amendment freedoms and the vital place they play in our democratic society. Certainly, the eloquent essays written by Justices Black and Douglas in the wake of earlier opinions by Holmes and Brandeis strike a responsive note in terms of the place of these freedoms in our open society and demonstrate the utility also of a theory of freedom that permits the widest exchange of ideas as the life blood of a democratic society.

It is understandable, however, that a majority of the Court, mindful of the ultimate responsibility of Congress for determining national policy and enacting appropriate measures for the national security, should be reluctant to engage in a head-on collision with Congress on these issues. Over the long run, as our constitutional history demonstrates, dominant forces of public opinion will play their part in constitutional interpretation. As has been suggested, the Court best performs its functions when it nudges and pulls at Congress rather than coming squarely to battle with it. And it may also be suggested that the greatest function the Court can perform in these cases, where free speech is an issue, is to employ its power of statutory interpretation and its review of concrete cases in a way that will maximize free speech and limit the operation of restrictive statutes. The importance of this function should not be underestimated, although it is too often obscured by debate and discussion of ultimate questions of constitutional power. By a careful and restrictive interpretation of statutes impinging on First Amendment freedoms and by its own review of the record as well as by the insistence upon scrupulous observance of procedural regularities, the Court can make a very effective contribution to the maintenance of these freedoms without precipitating a direct conflict with Congress. The Court can hold the Smith Act constitutional and still give its provisions a restrictive interpretation. It can uphold a broad investigative power by Congress and still find that a committee has not been authorized to act in a particular way or to inquire into a particular matter. In case of statutory ambiguity, it can resolve the doubts in favor of a construction that avoids a constitutional issue. Thus, in the case arising under the knowing membership clause of the Smith Act, the Court might well have found that Congress by a provision in the Internal Security Act had intended to grant immunity to members of the Communist Party from criminal liability based on party membership. Finally, in view of the grounds and theories of statutory interpretation relied upon to sustain the convictions in *Dennis* and *Scales,* the question could well be raised whether the defendants in these cases were properly apprised at the time of indictment and trial of the nature of the offense charged against them.

It is clear that we have adequate vehicles at present for dealing with Communists. Whether the statutes and other measures directed against them represent a wise or necessary use of governmental power is another question. That these measures are constitutional does not answer the question whether they are wise measures. Full exposure of Communism and its techniques and objectives serves a vital and useful purpose. But the usefulness or even desirability of criminal prosecutions under the Smith Act as a means of combating Communism is another matter. No one can doubt the seriousness of the threat that Communism presents to the free and democratic society we cherish. This is a global problem. Mr. Khrushchev predicts the collapse and burial of our type of society. Whether this expectation will be realized will depend not on whether we put a few Communists in jail but on the vitality and strength of our democratic system. Communism thrives on ignorance, poverty, and oppression. Rather than proceed from fear in our tactics and running the risk of driving domestic Communists underground, we do much better to proceed on a positive basis and challenge Communism in the open market place of ideas. In this battle we serve our cause best by shoring up democracy at home, maintaining a system that respects human dignity, is responsive to human needs, honors the basic liberties and a man's freedom to pursue his way, to make his daily choices, and to achieve his potentialities in a free, open, and pluralistic society. Our loyalty and devotion to these values, joined with sensitivity to and compassion for all peoples struggling to escape poverty, disease, ignorance, and exploitation, and an active program of effective assistance in the realization of these objectives, are the weapons for the positive attack in the battle we face. We must give them a sharp cutting edge.

MR. JUSTICE HUGO L. BLACK

Plain Words and Constitutional Absolutes

Hugo L. Black was a Senator from Alabama before being appointed to the Supreme Court by Franklin D. Roosevelt in 1937. On April 14, 1962, the American Jewish Congress held a banquet in honor of his twenty-five years of service on the Supreme Court. The program for the occasion was a public interview with Justice Black, conducted by the late Professor Edmond Cahn of the New York University Law School. The focus of the unrehearsed interview, reprinted here in its entirety, was on Justice Black's interpretation of the free speech provision of the First Amendment. Justice Black will soon be celebrating his 30th year on the Court.

Cahn: Let me start by explaining the purpose of this interview. Two years ago, when you delivered your James Madison Lecture at New York University, you declared your basic attitude toward our Bill of Rights. This was the positive side of your constitutional philosophy. Tonight I propose we bring out the other side, that is, your answers to the people who disagree with and criticize your

From Edmond Cahn, "Mr. Justice Black and the First Amendment 'Absolutes': A Public Interview," *New York University Law Review* (June, 1962), Vol. 37, pp. 549–563. Reprinted by permission of New York University, copyright owner.

principles. The questions I will ask, most of them at least, will be based on the criticisms. As you know, I consider your answers so convincing that I want the public to have them.

Suppose we start with one of the key sentences in your James Madison Lecture where you said, "It is my belief that there *are* 'absolutes' in our Bill of Rights, and that they were put there on purpose by men who knew what words meant and meant their prohibitions to be 'absolutes.' " Will you please explain your reasons for this.

Justice Black: My first reason is that I believe the words do mean what they say. I have no reason to challenge the intelligence, integrity, or honesty of the men who wrote the First Amendment. Among those I call the great men of the world are Thomas Jefferson, James Madison, and various others who participated in formulating the ideas behind the First Amendment for this country and in writing it.

I learned a long time ago that there are affirmative and negative words. The beginning of the First Amendment is that "Congress shall make no law." I understand that it is rather old-fashioned and shows a slight naïveté to say that "no law" means no law. It is one of the most amazing things about the ingeniousness of the times that strong arguments are made, which *almost* convince me, that it is very foolish of me to think "no law" means no law. But what it *says* is "Congress shall make no law respecting an establishment of religion," and so on.

I have to be honest about it. I confess not only that I think the Amendment means what it says but also that I may be slightly influenced by the fact that I do not think Congress *should* make any law with respect to these subjects. That has become a rather bad confession to make in these days, the confession that one is actually for something because he believes in it.

Then we move on, and it says "or prohibiting the free exercise thereof." I have not always exercised myself in regard to religion as much as I should, or perhaps as much as all of you have. Nevertheless, I want to be able to do it when I want to do it. I do not want anybody who is my servant, who is my agent, elected by me and others like me, to tell me that I can or cannot do it. Of course, some will remark that that is too simple on my part. To them, all this discussion of mine is too simple, because I come back to saying that these few plain words actually mean what they say, and I know of no college professor or law school professor, outside of my friend, Professor Cahn here, and a few others, who could not write one hundred pages to show that the Amendment does not mean what it says.

Then I move on to the words "abridging the freedom of speech or of the press." It *says* Congress shall make no law doing that. What it *means*—according to a current philosophy that I do not share—is that Congress shall be able to make just such a law unless we judges object too strongly. One of the statements of that philosophy is that if it shocks us too much, then they cannot do it. But when I get down to the really basic reason why I believe that "no law" means no law, I presume it could come to this, that I took an obligation to support and defend the Constitution as I understand it. And being a rather backward country fellow, I understand it to mean what the words say. Gesticulations apart, I know of no way in the world to communicate ideas except by words. And if I were to talk at great length on the subject, I would still be saying—although I understand that some people say that I just say it and do not believe it—that I believe when our Founding Fathers, with their wisdom and patriotism, wrote this Amendment, they knew what they were talking about. They knew what history was behind them and they wanted to ordain in this country that Congress, elected by the people, should not tell the people what religion they should have or what they should believe or say or publish, and that is about it. It says "no law," and that is what I believe it means.

Cahn: Some of your colleagues would say that it is better to interpret the Bill of Rights so as to permit Congress to take what it considers reasonable steps to preserve the security of the nation even at some sacrifice of freedom of speech and association. Otherwise what will happen to the Nation and the Bill of Rights as well? What is your view of this?

Justice Black: I fully agree with them that the country should protect itself. It should protect itself in peace and in war. It should do whatever is necessary to preserve itself. But the question is: preserve what? And how?

It is not very much trouble for a dictator to know how it is best to preserve his government. He wants to stay in power, and the best way to stay in power is to have plenty of force behind him. He cannot stay in power without force. He is afraid of too much talk; it is dangerous for him. And he should be afraid, because dictators do not have a way of contributing very greatly to the happiness, joy, contentment, and prosperity of the plain, everyday citizen. Their business is to protect themselves. Therefore, they need an army; they need to be able to stop people from talking; they need to have one religion, and that is the religion they promulgate. Frequently in the past it has been the worship of the dictator himself. To preserve a dictatorship, you must be able to stifle thought, imprison the human mind and intellect.

I want this Government to protect itself. If there is any man in the United States who owes a great deal to this Government, I am that man. Seventy years ago, when I was a boy, perhaps no one who knew me thought I would ever get beyond the confines of the small country county in which I was born. There was no reason for them to suspect that I would. But we had a free country and the way was open for me. The Government and the people of the United States have been good to me. Of course, I want this country to do what will preserve it. I want it to be preserved as the kind of government it was intended to be. I would not desire to live at any place where my thoughts were under the suspicion of government and where my words could be censored by government, and where worship, whatever it was or wasn't, had to be determined by an officer of the government. That is not the kind of government I want preserved.

I agree with those who wrote our Constitution, that too much power in the hands of officials is a dangerous thing. What was government created for except to serve the people? Why was a Constitution written for the first time in this country except to limit the power of government and those who were selected to exercise it at the moment?

My answer to the statement that this Government should preserve itself is yes. The method I would adopt is different, however, from that of some other people. I think it can be preserved only by leaving people with the utmost freedom to think and to hope and to talk and to dream if they want to dream. I do not think this Government must look to force, stifling the minds and aspirations of the people. Yes, I believe in self-preservation, but I would preserve it as the Founders said, by leaving people free. I think here, as in another time, it cannot live half slave and half free.

Cahn: I do not suppose that since the days of Socrates a questioner ever got answers that were so co-operative.

In order to preserve the guaranteed freedom of the press, are you willing to allow sensational newspaper reports about a crime and about police investigation of the crime to go so far that they prejudice and inflame a whole state and thus deprive the accused of his right to a fair jury?

Justice Black: The question assumes in the first place that a whole state can be inflamed so that a fair trial is not possible. On most of these assumptions that are made with reference to the dangers of the spread of information, I perhaps diverge at a point from many of those who disagree with my views. I have again a kind of an old-fashioned trust in human beings. I learned it as a boy and have never wholly lost that faith.

I believe in trial by jury. Here again perhaps I am a literalist. I do not think that trial by jury is a perfect way of determining facts, of adjudicating guilt, or of adjudicating controversies. But I do not know of a better way. That is where I stand on that.

I do not think myself that any one can say that there can be enough publicity completely to destroy the ideas of fairness in the minds of people, including the judges. One of the great things about trials by jury in criminal cases that have developed in this country—I refer to criminal cases because there is where most of the persecutions are found in connection with bringing charges against unpopular people or people in unpopular causes—we should not forget that if the jury happens to go wrong, the judge has a solemn duty in a criminal case not to let an unfair verdict stand. Also, in this country, an appellate court can hear the case.

I realize that we do not have cases now like they had when William Penn was tried for preaching on the streets of London. The jury which was called in to send him off quickly to jail refused to do so, and suffered punishment from the judge because they would not convict a man for preaching on the streets. But that is a part of history, and it is but one of thousands of cases of the kind. Those people had publicity; that is why they would not convict William Penn. They knew, because the people had been talking, despite the fact that there was so much censorship then, that William Penn was being prosecuted largely because he was a dissenter from the orthodox views. So they stood up like men and would not convict. They lost their property, some of them their liberty. But they stood up like men.

I do not myself think that it is necessary to stifle the press in order to reach fair verdicts. Of course, we do not want juries to be influenced wrongfully. But with our system of education we should be in better condition than they were in those days in England, when they found that the jury was one of the greatest steps on their way to freedom. As a matter of fact, Madison placed trial by jury along with freedom of the press and freedom of conscience as the three most highly cherished liberties of the American people in his time.

I do not withdraw my loyalty to the First Amendment or say that the press should be censored on the theory that in order to preserve fair trials it is necessary to try the people of the press in summary contempt proceedings and send them to jail for what they have published. I want both fair trials and freedom of the press. I grant that you cannot get everything you want perfectly, and you never will. But you won't do any good in this country, which aspires to freedom, by saying just give the courts a little more power, just a little more power to suppress the people and the press and things will be all right. You just take a little chunk off here and little bit there. I would not take it off anywhere. I believe that they meant what they said about freedom of the press just as they meant what they said about establishment of religion, and I would answer this question as I have answered the other one.

Cahn: Do you make an exception in freedom of speech and press for the law of defamation? That is, are you willing to allow people to sue for damages when they are subjected to libel or slander?

Justice Black: My view of the First Amendment, as originally ratified, is that it said Congress should pass none of these kinds of laws. As written at that time, the Amendment applied only to Congress. I have no doubt myself that the provision, as written and adopted, intended that there should be no libel or defamation law in the United States under the United States Government, just absolutely none so far as I am concerned.

That is, no federal law. At that time—I will have to state this in order to let you know what I think about libel and defamation—people were afraid of the new Federal Government. I hope that they have not wholly lost that fear up to this time because, while government is a wonderful and an essential thing in order to have any kind of liberty, order or peace, it has such power that people must always remember to check them here and balance them there and limit them here in order to see that you do not lose too much liberty in exchange for government. So I have no doubt about what the Amendment intended. As a matter of fact, shortly after the Constitution was written, a man named St. George Tucker, a great friend of Madison's, who served as one of the commissioners at the Annapolis convention of 1786 which first attempted to fill the need for a national constitution, put out a revised edition of Blackstone. In it he explained what our Constitution meant with reference to freedom of speech and press. He said there was no doubt in his mind, as one of the earliest participants in the development of the Constitution, that it was intended that there should be no libel under the laws of the United States. Lawyers might profit from consulting Tucker's edition of Blackstone on that subject.

As far as public libel is concerned, or seditious libel, I have been very much disturbed sometimes to see that there is present an idea that because we have had the practice of suing individuals for libel, seditious libel still remains for the use of government in this country. Seditious libel, as it has been put into practice throughout the centuries, is nothing in the world except the prosecution of people who are on the wrong side politically; they have said something and their group has lost and they are prosecuted. Those of you who read the newspaper see that this is happening all over the world now, every week somewhere. Somebody gets out, somebody else gets in, they call a military court or a special commission, and they try him. When he gets through sometimes he is not living.

My belief is that the First Amendment was made applicable to the states by the Fourteenth. I do not hesitate, so far as my own view is concerned, as to what should be and what I hope will sometime be the constitutional doctrine that just as it was not intended to authorize damage suits for mere words as distinguished from conduct as far as the Federal Government is concerned, the same rule should apply to the states.

I realize that sometimes you have a libel suit that accomplishes some good. I practiced law twenty years. I was a pretty active trial lawyer. The biggest judgment I ever got for a libel was $300. I never took a case for political libel because I found out that Alabama juries, at least, do not believe in political libel suits and they just do not give verdicts. I knew of one verdict given against a big newspaper down there for $25,000, and the Supreme Court of Alabama reversed it. So even that one did not pan out very well.

I believe with Jefferson that it is time enough for government to step in to regulate people when they *do* something, not when they *say* something, and I do not believe myself that there is *any* halfway ground if you enforce the protections of the First Amendment.

Cahn: Would it be constitutional to prosecute someone who falsely shouted "fire" in a theater?

Justice Black: I went to a theater last night with you. I have an idea if you and I had gotten up and marched around that theater, whether we said anything or not, we would have been arrested. Nobody has ever said that the First Amendment gives people a right to go anywhere in the world they want to go or say anything in the world they want to say. Buying the theater tickets did not buy the opportunity to make a speech there. We have a system of property in this country which is also protected by the Constitution. We have a system of property, which means that a man does not have a right to do anything he wants anywhere he wants to do it. For instance, I would feel a little badly if somebody were to try to come into my house and tell me that he had a constitutional right to come in there because he wanted to make a speech against the Supreme Court. I realize the freedom of people to make a speech against the Supreme Court, but I do not want him to make it in my house.

That is a wonderful aphorism about shouting "fire" in a crowded theater. But you do not have to shout "fire" to get arrested. If a person creates a disorder in a theater, they would get him there not because of *what* he hollered but because he *hollered.* They would get him not because of any views he had but because they thought he did not have any views that they wanted to hear there. That is the way I would answer: not because of what he shouted but because he shouted.

Cahn: Is there any kind of obscene material, whether defined as hard-core pornography or otherwise, the distribution and sale of which can be constitutionally restricted in any manner whatever, in your opinion?

Justice Black: I will say it can in this country, because the courts have held that it can.

Cahn: Yes, but you won't get off so easily. I want to know what you think.

Justice Black: My view is, without deviation, without exception, without any ifs, buts, or whereases, that freedom of speech means that you shall not do something to people either for the views they have or the views they express or the words they speak or write.

There is strong argument for the position taken by a man whom I admire very greatly, Dr. Meiklejohn, that the First Amendment really was intended to protect *political* speech, and I do think that was the basic purpose; that plus the fact that they wanted to protect *religious* speech. Those were the two main things they had in mind.

It is the law that there can be an arrest made for obscenity. It was the law in Rome that they could arrest people for obscenity after Augustus became Caesar. Tacitus says that then it became obscene to criticize the Emperor. It is not any trouble to establish a classification so that whatever it is that you do not want said is within that classification. So far as I am concerned, I do not believe there is any halfway ground for protecting freedom of speech and press. If you say it is half free, you can rest assured that it will not remain as much as half free. Madison explained that in his great Remonstrance when he said in effect, "If you make laws to force people to speak the words of Christianity, it won't be long until the same power will narrow the sole religion to the most powerful sect in it." I realize that there are dangers in freedom of speech, but I do not believe there are any halfway marks.

Cahn: Do you subscribe to the idea involved in the clear and present danger rule?

Justice Black: I do not.

Cahn: By way of conclusion, Justice Black, would you kindly summarize what you consider the judge's role in cases arising under the First Amendment and the Bill of Rights?

Justice Black: The Bill of Rights to me constitutes the difference between this country and many others. I will not attempt to say most others or nearly all others or all others. But I will say it constitutes the difference to me between a free country and a country that is not free.

My idea of the whole thing is this: There has been a lot of trouble in the world between people and government. The people were afraid of government; they had a right to be afraid. All over the world men had been destroyed—and when I say "government" I mean the individuals who actually happened to be in control of it at the moment, whether they were elected, whether they were appointed, whether they got there with the sword, however they got there—the people always had a lot of trouble because power is a heady thing, a dangerous thing. There have been very few individuals in the history of the world who could be trusted with complete, unadulterated, omnipotent power over their fellowmen.

Millions of people have died throughout the world because of the evils of their governments. Those days had not wholly passed when the Pilgrims came over to this country. Many of them had suffered personally. Some of them had their ears cut off. Many of them had been mutilated. Many of their ancestors had. Some of your ancestors came here to get away from persecution. Certainly, mine did.

There had been struggles throughout the ages to curb the dangerous power of governors. Rome had a sound government at one time. Those who study it carefully will find that, except for the slave class, they had, so far as most of the people were concerned, a good form of government. But it turned, and then they had Augustus and the other Caesars, and the Neros and Caligulas and Tiberiuses.

One of the interesting things about Tiberius is that in all the history I have read he is about the only man of great prominence who ever defended informers. He made the statement that the informers were the guardians of Rome. Recently I have heard that said here once or twice.

When our ancestors came over here and started this country, they had some more persecutions of their own. It was not limited to any one religion. A lot of my Baptist brethren got into trouble; a lot of the Methodist brethren got in trouble; a lot of the Episcopal Church got in trouble, the Congregational Church—each of them in turn. A lot of the Catholics got in trouble. Whichever sect was in control in a state for a time, they would say that the others could not hold office, which is an easy way of getting rid of your adversaries if you can put it over. Even for half a century after the Constitution was adopted, some of the States barred the members of certain faiths from holding office.

Throughout all of this—as the Jewish people know as well as any people on earth—persecutions were abroad everywhere in the world. A man never knew, when he got home, whether his family would be there, and the family at home never knew whether the head of the family would get back. There was nothing strange about that when Hitler did it. It was simply a repetition of the course of history when people get too much power.

I like what the Jewish people did when they took what amounted to a written constitution. Some of the states did it before the time of the Federal Constitution; they adopted written constitutions. Why? Because they wanted to mark boundaries beyond which government could not go, stripping people of their liberty to think, to talk, to write, to work, to be happy.

So we have a written Constitution. What good is it? What good is it if, as some judges say, all it means is: "Government, you can still do this unless it is so bad that it shocks the conscience of the judges." It does not say that to me. We have certain provisions in the Constitution which say, "Thou shalt not." They do not say, "You can do this unless it offends the sense of decency of the English-speaking world." They do not say that. They do not say, "You can go ahead and do this unless it is offensive to the universal sense of decency." If they did, they would say virtually nothing. There would be no definite, binding place, no specific prohibition, if that were all it said.

I believe with Locke in the system of checks and balances. I do not think that the Constitution leaves any one department of government free without there being a check on it somewhere. Of course, things are different in England; they do have unchecked powers, and they also have a very impressive history. But it was *not* the kind of history that suited the people that formed our Constitution. Madison said that explicitly when he offered the Bill of Rights to the Congress. Jefferson repeated it time and time again. Why was it not? Because it left Parliament with power to pass such laws as it saw fit to pass. It was not the kind of government they wanted. So we have a Bill of Rights. It is intended to see that a man cannot be jerked by the back of the neck by any government official; he cannot have his home invaded; he cannot be picked up legally and carried away because his views are not satisfactory to the majority, even if they are terrible views, however bad they may be. Our system of justice is based on the assumption that men can best work out their own opinions, and that they are not under the control of government. Of course, this is particularly true in the field of religion, because a man's religion is between himself and his Creator, not between himself and his government.

I am not going to say any more except this: I was asked a question about preserving this country. I confess I am a complete chauvinist. I think it is the greatest country in the world. I think it is the greatest because it has a Bill of Rights. I think it could be the worst if it did not have one. It does not take a nation long to degenerate. We saw, only a short time ago, a neighboring country where people were walking the streets in reasonable peace one day and within a month we saw them marched to the back of a wall to meet a firing squad without a trial.

I am a chauvinist because this country offers the greatest opportunities of any country in the world to people of every kind, of every type, of every race, of every origin, of every religion—without regard to wealth, without regard to poverty. It offers an opportunity to the child born today to be reared among his people by his people, to worship his God, whatever his God may be, or to refuse to worship anybody's God if that is his wish. It is a free country; it will remain free only, however, if we recognize that the boundaries of freedom are not so flexible; they are not made of mush. They say, "Thou shalt not," and I think that is what they mean.

Now, I have read that every sophisticated person knows that you cannot have any absolute "thou shalt nots." But you know when I drive my car against a red light, I do not expect them to turn me loose if I can prove that though I was going across that red light, it was not offensive to the so-called "universal sense of decency." I have an idea there are some absolutes. I do not think I am far in that respect from the Holy Scriptures.

The Jewish people have had a glorious history. It is wonderful to think about the contributions that were made to the world from a small, remote area in the East. I have to admit that most of my ideas stem basically from there.

It is largely because of these same contributions that I am here tonight as a member of what I consider the greatest Court in the world. It is great because it is independent. If it were not independent, it would not be great. If all nine of those men came out each Monday morning like a phonograph speaking one voice, you could rest assured it would not be independent. But it does not come that way. I want to assure you that the fact that it does not come that way does not mean that there is not a good, sound, wholesome respect on the part of every Justice for every other Justice.

I do hope that this occasion may cause you to think a little more and study a little more about the Constitution, which is the source of your liberty; no, not the source—I will take that back—but a protection of your liberty. Yesterday a man sent me a copy of a recent speech entitled "Is the First Amendment Obsolete?" The conclusion of the writer, who is a distinguished law school dean, was that the Amendment no longer fits the times and that it needs to be modified to get away from its rigidity. The author contends that the thing to do is to take the term "due process of law" and measure everything by that standard, "due process of law" meaning that unless a law is so bad that it shocks the conscience of the Court, it cannot be unconstitutional. I do not wish to have to pass on the laws of this country according to the degree of shock I receive! Some people get shocked more readily than others at certain things. I get shocked pretty quickly, I confess, when I see—and this I say with trepidation because it is considered bad to admit it—but I do get shocked now and then when I see some gross injustice has been done, although I am solemnly informed that we do not sit to administer justice, we sit to administer law in the abstract.

I am for the First Amendment from the first word to the last. I believe it means what it says, and it says to me: "Government shall keep its hands off religion. Government shall not attempt to control the ideas a man has. Government shall not attempt to establish a religion of any kind. Government shall not abridge freedom of the press or speech. It shall let anybody talk in this country." I have never been shaken in the faith that the American people are the kind of people and have the kind of loyalty to their government that we need not fear the talk of Communists or of anybody else. Let them talk! In the American way, we will answer them.

SIDNEY HOOK

A Philosopher Dissents in the Case of Absolutes

Sidney Hook is a professor of philosophy at New York University. In the selection below, he sternly criticizes the absolutist position of Justice Black: "Justice Black is under the illusion that his doctrinaire extremism is a bulwark of our freedom. . . . The truth is that if his views became the law of the land . . . the entire structure of our freedoms would go down in dust and turmoil."

From Sidney Hook, "Lord Monboddo and the Supreme Court." Reprinted with permission from the author and from *The New Leader* of May 13, 1963, pp. 11-15. Copyright The American Labor Conference on International Affairs, Inc.

"The most important thing about a judge," Professor Paul Freund has wisely observed, "is his philosophy; and if it be dangerous for him to have one, it is at all events less dangerous than the self-deception of not having one."

No one can read this collection of Justice Hugo Black's opinions without becoming aware of the overriding importance of his philosophy. It is more in evidence than judicial reasoning based on legal principle and precedent. For most judges it is only when the texts and resources of the law, the rules of evidence, and the facts in the case are insufficient to point clearly to a decision that what Holmes called "can't helps," and Freund "ultimate convictions or values," show themselves—and even then by indirection. In Justice Black's opinions, however, his "can't helps" lie on the surface. His opinions follow from them almost automatically.

Fortunately, the editor has opened and closed the collection with two statements of Black's views. The first is a lecture on the Bill of Rights. The second is the verbatim text of his answers to questions put to him by an admiring interlocutor in a public interview. They are forceful expressions of Justice Black's basic philosophy, and are highly commendable for their frankness.

Since Black insists upon his words being taken in the same literal sense with which he believes he interprets the words of the Constitution, readers whose minds have not been drugged by rhetoric will find his views startling both for their intellectual simplicity and practical extremism. Indeed, the implications of Black's articulated philosophy are so terrifying that if it were to prevail, the entire structure of human freedom would be more seriously undermined than if the legislative measures he deplores were multiplied a thousand times over. For Justice Black would strip American citizens of any legal protection against every form of slander, libel and defamation, no matter how grave and irreparable the consequent damage to life, limb, property and reputation. The very foundations of civil society—and not merely of democratic society, whose viability depends more than any other on certain standards of public virtue—would collapse if speech which falsely charged citizens with murder, theft, rape, arson and treason was regarded as public discussion and hence privileged under the law.

It may be instructive to examine the assumptions from which Justice Black derives his position. Most jurists are very sensitive to the charge of absolutism, for an absolutist, like a fanatic, is one who refuses to test his principles in the light of reason and experience, and explore alternatives to what may be no more than arbitrary prejudices tricked out as self-evident axioms or convictions. Justice Black, however, is proud of his absolutism with respect to the Bill of Rights. The starting point of his public colloquy is the emphatic reassertion that "there are 'absolutes' in our Bill of Rights and that they were put there on purpose by men who knew what words meant and meant their prohibitions to be 'absolutes.' "

Now there are obvious and elementary difficulties with the notion of rights being so absolute that they can never be legitimately abridged. The first difficulty is that it makes intellectually incoherent the acceptance of certain laws whose justice is acknowledged even by alleged believers in absolute rights. For example, the First Amendment forbids the making of any law "prohibiting the free exercise" of religion. As everyone knows, some religions involve morally objectionable practices ranging from polygamy to human sacrifice, all of which are forbidden by law. Simple consistency would require absolutists to deny to Congress or any other legislative body the right to proscribe the exercise of such religions. But as far as I know all absolutists, on the bench or off, approve of these laws.

The difficulty in the absolutists' position, although formidable, is not insuperable. For theoretically the absolutist of religious freedom can always abandon his rejection of inhuman or morally objectionable religious practices and in principle declare for the toleration of any religious practice. Cicero somewhere asserts that there is no absurdity to which some human beings will not resort to defend another absurdity. Those who make an absolute of the free exercise of religion or any other right will not necessarily be brought up short by the realization of the absurdity of their position if they are prepared to swallow all its consequences.

The second elementary difficulty with the doctrine of absolute rights, however, *is* insuperable. One of the commonest experiences in life is the conflict of rights. But if rights are absolute how can there be more than one of them? In this respect, rights are like the obligation to keep a promise. If promises conflict, how can we believe that *all* promises must be kept? Suppose the right to speak interferes, as it very well might, with the free exercise of someone else's religion—which one must be abridged? Or suppose, to relate the discussion to Justice Black's own text, that freedom of speech or press conflicts with a man's right to a fair trial?

Justice Black explicitly states that he wants "both fair trials and freedom of the press." He agrees with Madison that "trial by jury along with freedom of the press and freedom of conscience [are] the three most highly cherished liberties of the American people." Very well. What happens when a newspaper publishes, or a station broadcasts, so highly inflammatory an account of a crime and of an arrested suspect that it prejudices the latter's right to a fair trial by a jury? Black's reply to the question is that this *never* occurs. He does not believe it possible for a state to be so inflamed by press or radio as to prejudice a man's right to a fair trial. I think his reply is irrelevant because it avoids giving a direct answer to the hypothetical question. Even if we did not know of a situation in which a conflict like this has arisen, we could easily conceive of one. Which right should yield?

But we do not have to conceive of such a situation as if it were merely a fancied possibility. Very often motions for a change of venue are granted, among other reasons, on the ground that press reports have been prejudicial to the defendant. A newspaper often has state-wide circulation, and a radio station frequently reaches an audience in every village and hamlet in a state. Black's reply seems blithe as well as irrelevant because it substitutes his subjective impression for an entire encyclopedia of authenticated facts in legal history.

"I do not think myself," he says, "that anyone can say there can be enough publicity completely to destroy the ideas of fairness in the minds of people, including judges." Note the use of the word "completely." What can be established "completely" in law or life? If only one man remains unprejudiced by an incendiary editorial urging that a defendant be legally lynched, does that mean that a fair trial is possible? One or more persons may be unprejudiced and yet every person on the jury as well as the judge may have been profoundly influenced by tendentious press or radio reports.

A trial is unfair even if only some member or members of a jury have been prejudiced by what they have read. The wisdom of the law has no place for complete or final or absolute proof in matters of this sort. It recognizes that even when a man's very life is at stake we cannot forego reaching a verdict merely because the conclusion is less than certain. It is sufficient to reach conclusions that are beyond reasonable doubt. There are many cases in which there can be no reasonable doubt that the press treatment of a crime and of a suspect has prejudiced the defendant's right to a fair trial. When that happens, which of the two freedoms in conflict should be abridged?

An idea becomes a dogma when it blinds one to the facts of experience. The more important the recognition of these facts is to the intelligent defense of human liberty, the more dangerous these dogmas become. Were Black's position to become the dominant view of the United States Supreme Court, its effects on the already irresponsible practices of the sensationalist press in reporting criminal cases would be fearful to contemplate. The English public is far freer from racial, religious and sectional prejudice than the American public. Yet everyone knows how jealously the rights of a defendant in a criminal case are safeguarded in England. Neither the press nor the radio feels muzzled because its freedom to comment on a criminal case before the verdict is rendered is not absolute.

Justice Black refuses to admit the possibility that freedom of speech may conflict with the right to a fair trial. Nonetheless, his altogether unconvincing attempt to explain away the conflict reveals that despite what he says, he does *not* believe in the absolute right to a fair trial. In cases of actual conflict he would rule, apparently on purely *a priori* grounds, that the right to speech or press must be upheld whatever its consequences for other rights, especially the right of an individual not to be prejudiced by his judges.

This creates another difficulty for him even more obvious and formidable than the ones we have considered. In developing their doctrine of "clear and present danger" as a rule which governs limitations on speech and press, Justices Holmes and Brandeis were wont to use some specific illustrations which have until now seemed very plausible to common sense. Black has no use for the doctrine of "clear and present danger," but he recognizes one of Holmes' illustrations as a challenge to his position. In his famous opinion in *Schenck vs. U.S.*, Holmes wrote: "The most stringent protection of free speech would not protect a man in falsely shouting 'fire' in a theatre, and causing a panic." The illustration has become a paradigm case of the kind of speech which is not legally protected and morally should not be.

Justice Black's friendly questioner, Professor Edmond Cahn, with this paradigm case in mind, asked him: "Would it be constitutional to prosecute someone who falsely shouted 'fire' in a theatre?" To which Justice Black replied affirmatively but *not* for the reasons Holmes gives. Such a man would be prosecuted, he asserts, "not because of what he shouted but because he shouted." Black explains:

"Nobody has ever said that the First Amendment gives people a right to go anywhere in the world they want to go or say anything in the world they want to say. Buying theatre tickets did not buy the opportunity to make a speech there. We have a system of property in this country which is also protected by the Constitution . . .

"That is a wonderful aphorism about shouting 'fire' in a crowded theatre. But you do not have to shout 'fire' to get arrested. If a person creates a disorder in a theatre, they would get him there not because of *what* he hollered but because he *hollered*." (Italics in original.)

This is a permanent contribution to the humor of the law! Suppose someone falsely shouted "fire," not in a theater but in a church or school or a public place where there is no question of the right of property. Would the shout then be privileged? And if *what* a person hollers is irrelevant but the mere *fact* that he hollered justifies prosecution, suppose he hollers "fire" in a crowded theater, and it is true. There *is* a fire! Would Black hold that he should be arrested for creating a disturbance, that *what* he shouted was irrelevant?

The law would be an ass if it failed to take account of *what* a person shouted. For in that case it could not distinguish between the man who shouted "fire" falsely and one who shouted "fire" when there really was one. The effects of the shout depend almost entirely upon the meaning of the words shouted.

The law would be doubly asinine if it treated shouts of "fire" merely as forms of disorderly conduct whether or not there was a fire, and independently of the intent of the shouter. But it does no such thing. If panic and death resulted from a knowingly false shout of "fire," say in order to facilitate pickpocketing or to get "kicks" out of watching the frenzied rush to safety, the malefactor might be subject to a charge of manslaughter. On the other hand, a truthful shout of "fire," even if it were unwise, would not be actionable.

One can, of course, knowingly shout many things in a theater that are false without incurring the penalties which would follow on the normal consequences of falsely shouting something that would cause a riot. No one is arrested for disorderly conduct for shouting barefaced lies about the great talent or beauty of the performers. If we disregard the meaning and intent of what a man hollers, none of these distinctions can be drawn.

Despite the absurdity of Justice Black's attempt to square his position with the judgments of common sense, he seems unaware of the fact that he has breached the absoluteness of the right to speak when its exercise interferes with the right to property which, as he reminds us, is also protected by the Constitution. Holmes' rule limits freedom of speech when it incites to illegal violence or when it threatens life, as does the false cry of "fire" in the theater. Justice Black apparently would limit freedom of speech only when its expression is a trespass on private property. It is a fair inference from his dissenting opinion in *Yates vs. United States* that he would not penalize speech about a public issue which incites to an illegal action like lynching. ("I believe," he wrote, "that the First Amendment forbids Congress to punish people for talking about public affairs, whether or not such discussion incites to action legal or illegal.") But is not the right to life more precious than the right to property and the right to speech?

One would imagine that with these remarks Black has reached the limits of doctrinaire extremism. Yet he has another surprise in store for us. Not only does he hold—by a remarkably original feat of constitutional reinterpretation—that the First Amendment forbids all libel or defamation laws, but he asserts that since the First Amendment was made applicable to the states by the Fourteenth, this should be the general rule valid everywhere:

"I have no doubt that the provision [the First Amendment] as written and adopted, intended that there should be no libel or defamation law in the United States under the United States Government, just absolutely none so far as I am concerned . . .

"My belief is that the First Amendment was made applicable to the states by the Fourteenth. I do not hesitate, so far as my view is concerned, as to what should be and what I hope will sometime be the constitutional doctrine that just as it was not intended to authorize damage suits for mere words as distinguished from conduct as far as the Federal Government is concerned, the same rule should apply to the states."

This means that if one falsely charges a person in a position of trust with being an embezzler, or charges a scholar with plagiarism, or a teacher with perverse abuse of his students or an official with handing over secret documents to enemy agents, or a nurse with poisoning a patient (to mention only a few notorious cases in recent years), and that as a consequence of these false and malicious charges the innocent person's professional life has been ruined, the victim can have no redress from the calumniator. It is only a matter of words, not of actions, says Justice Black.

This means, also, that if one falsely charges that the butcher or grocer is using dishonest scales or selling deceptively packaged meat and foodstuffs which have been officially condemned as unfit for human consumption, and that in consequence an honest merchant suffers irreparable damage, he cannot sue the architect of his ruin. Here again it is only a matter of words, not of actions. One wonders what has happened to the right of property previously recognized by Black.

This means, finally, that if a racist and anti-Semite not merely accused Jews as a group of ritual blood murder but accuses a specific Jew of the ritual blood murder of a missing non-Jewish child, or a specific Negro of a specific unsolved crime against a white, and the Jew or Negro suffers acutely in consequence, there can be no redress at law against this criminal and wicked libel. It, too, is only a matter of words, not of actions.

All of this goes four-square against the grain of Anglo-American law, which permits not only a civil suit for damages if a man has been libelled but sometimes also a criminal prosecution. It runs counter to the humane legal tradition which allows truth to be a legitimate defense in a civil action for damages, but refuses to accept even the truth as a legitimate defense in an action for criminal libel if it can be shown that the charge was made with a malicious intent which served no good public end. It outrages the moral sensibility of those who believe that their good name or honor "is the immediate jewel of their souls," more precious to them than the size of their purse. . . .

Justice Black is under the illusion that his doctrinaire extremism is a bulwark of our freedom, especially of the strategic freedoms of the Bill of Rights. The truth is that if his views became the law of the land, and the citizens of our republic could libel and slander each other with complete impunity, democratic self-government would be impossible and the entire structure of our freedoms would go down in dust and turmoil.

If views such as these were held by a judge of an inferior court, they could be dismissed as a quaint peccadillo. When they are held with passionate conviction by a distinguished and influential Justice of the highest court in the land, a Supreme Court which often functions as a third legislative body, they should be a cause of grave concern to all who cherish the ideals of multiple freedoms under law. They should give especial pause to those who believe it is possible to make absolutes out of any particular freedom, or, in other words, who wish to be liberal without being intelligent.

III Freedom of Expression in an Age of Protest

PUBLIC OFFICIALS AND THE LAW OF LIBEL

MR. JUSTICE WILLIAM J. BRENNAN, JR.

Maintaining Wide-open and Robust Public Debate

William Brennan was appointed to the Supreme Court in 1956 by President Eisenhower. In 1964, Justice Brennan delivered the decision in the New York Times *case, in which the Court substantially modified the law under which public officials could bring libel suits against newspapers. "The constitutional guarantees require," he wrote, ". . . a federal rule that prohibits a public official from recovering damages for a defamatory falsehood relating to his official conduct . . ." unless he can show that it was made with ". . . knowledge that it was false or with reckless disregard of whether it was false or not." Behind the decision lay the argument that "debate on public issues should be uninhibited, robust, and wide-open. . . ."*

WE ARE REQUIRED FOR THE FIRST TIME in this case to determine the extent to which the constitutional protections for speech and press limit a State's power to award damages in a libel action brought by a public official against critics of his official conduct.

Respondent L. B. Sullivan is one of the three elected Commissioners of the City of Montgomery, Alabama. He testified that he was

Justice William J. Brennan, Jr. speaking for the majority in *New York Times v. Sullivan,* 376 U. S. 254 (1964). Case citations omitted.

"Commissioner of Public Affairs and the duties are supervision of the Police Department, Fire Department, Department of Cemetery and Department of Scales." He brought this civil libel action against the four individual petitioners, who are Negroes and Alabama clergymen, and against petitioner the New York Times Company, a New York corporation which publishes the New York Times, a daily newspaper. A jury in the Circuit Court of Montgomery County awarded him damages of $500,000, the full amount claimed, against all the petitioners, and the Supreme Court of Alabama affirmed.

Respondents complaint alleged that he had been libeled by statements in a full-page advertisement that was carried in the New York Times on March 29, 1960. Entitled "Heed Their Rising Voices," the advertisement began by stating that "As the whole world knows by now, thousands of Southern Negro students are engaged in widespread non-violent demonstrations in positive affirmation of the right to live in human dignity as guaranteed by the U. S. Constitution and the Bill of Rights." It went on to charge that "in their efforts to uphold these guarantees, they are being met by an unprecedented wave of terror by those who would deny and negate that document which the whole world looks upon as setting the pattern for modern freedom. . . ." Succeeding paragraphs purported to illustrate the "wave of terror" by describing certain alleged events. The text concluded with an appeal for funds for three purposes: support of the student movement, "the struggle for the right-to-vote," and the legal defense of Dr. Martin Luther King, Jr., leader of the movement, against a perjury indictment then pending in Montgomery. . . .

It is uncontroverted that some of the statements contained in the two paragraphs were not accurate descriptions of events which occurred in Montgomery. Although Negro students staged a demonstration on the State Capitol steps, they sang the National Anthem and not "My Country, 'Tis of Thee." Although nine students were expelled by the State Board of Education, this was not for leading the demonstration at the Capitol, but for demanding service at a lunch counter in the Montgomery County Courthouse on another day. Not the entire student body, but most of it, had protested the expulsion, not by refusing to register, but by boycotting classes on a single day; virtually all the students did register for the ensuing semester. The campus dining hall was not padlocked on any occasion, and the only students who may have been barred from eating there were the few who had neither signed a preregistration application nor requested temporary meal tickets. Although the police were deployed near the campus in large numbers on three occasions, they did not at any time "ring" the campus, and they were not called to the campus in connection with the demonstration on the State Capitol steps, as the third paragraph implied. Dr. King had not been arrested seven times, but only four; and although he claimed to have been assaulted some years earlier in connection with his arrest for loitering outside a courtroom, one of the officers who made the arrest denied that there was such an assault. . . .

Because of the importance of the constitutional issues involved, we granted the separate petitions for certiorari of the individual petitioners and of the Times. . . . We reverse the judgment. We hold that the rule of law applied by the Alabama courts is constitutionally deficient for failure to provide the safeguards for freedom of speech and of the press that are required by the First and Fourteenth Amendments in a libel action brought by a public official against critics of his official conduct. We further hold that under the proper safeguards the evidence presented in this case is constitutionally insufficient to support the judgment for respondent. . . .

Thus we consider this case against the background of a profound national commitment to the principle that debate on public issues should be uninhibited, robust, and wide-open, and that it may well include vehement, caustic, and sometimes unpleasantly sharp attacks on government and public officials. . . . The present advertisement, as an expression of grievance and protest on one of the major public issues of our time, would seem clearly to qualify for the constitutional protection. The question is whether it forfeits that protection by the falsity of some of its factual statements and by its alleged defamation of respondent.

Authoritative interpretations of the First Amendment guarantees have consistently refused to recognize an exception for any test of truth, whether administered by judges, juries, or administrative officials—and especially not one that puts the burden of proving truth on the speaker. . . . The constitutional protection does not turn upon "the truth, popularity, or social utility of the ideas and beliefs which are offered. . . ."

That erroneous statement is inevitable in free debate, and that it must be protected if the freedoms of expression are to have the "breathing space" that they "need . . . to survive, . . ." was also recognized by the Court of Appeals for the District of Columbia Circuit in Sweeney v. Patterson. . . . Judge Edgerton spoke for a unanimous court which affirmed the dismissal of a Congressman's libel suit based upon a newspaper article charging him with anti-Semitism in opposing a judicial appointment. . . .

Just as factual error affords no warrant for repressing speech that would otherwise be free, the same is true of injury to official reputation. Where judicial officers are involved, this Court has held that concern for the dignity and reputation of the courts does not justify the punishment as criminal contempt of criticism of the judge or his decision. . . . This is true even though the utterance contains "half-truths" and "misinformation. . . ." If judges are to be treated as "men of fortitude, able to thrive in a hardy climate, . . ." surely the same must be true of other government officials, such as elected city commissioners. Criticism of their official conduct does not lose its constitutional protection merely because it is effective criticism and hence diminishes their official reputations.

If neither factual error nor defamatory content suffices to remove the constitutional shield from criticism of official conduct, the combination of the two elements is no less inadequate. This is the lesson to be drawn from the great controversy over the Sedition Act of 1798, . . . which first crystallized a national awareness of the central meaning of the First Amendment. . . . That statute made it a crime, punishable by a $5,000 fine and five years in prison, "if any person shall write, print, utter or publish . . . any false, scandalous and malicious writing or writings against the government of the United States, or either house of the Congress . . ., or the President . . ., with the intent to defame . . . or to bring them or either of them, into contempt or disrepute; or to excite against them, or either or any of them, the hatred of the good people of the United States." The Act allowed the defendant the defense of truth, and provided that the jury were to be judges both of the law and the facts. Despite these qualifications, the Act was vigorously condemned as unconstitutional in an attack joined in by Jefferson and Madison. In the famous Virginia Resolutions of 1798, the General Assembly of Virginia resolved that it "doth particularly protest against the palpable and alarming infractions of the Constitution, in the two late cases of the 'Alien and Sedition Acts,' passed at the last session of Congress . . . . Congress [The Sedition Act] exercises . . . a power not delegated by the Constitution, but, on the contrary, expressly and positively forbidden by one of the amendments thereto—a power which, more than any other, ought to produce universal alarm, because it is levelled against the right of freely examining public characters and measures, and of free communication among the people thereon, which has ever been justly deemed the only effectual guardian of every other right. . . ."

Madison prepared the Report in support of the protest. His premise was that the Constitution created a form of government under which "The people, not the government, possess the absolute sovereignty." The structure of the government dispersed power in reflection of the people's distrust of concentrated power, and of power itself at all levels. This form of government was "altogether different" from the British form, under which the Crown was sovereign and the people were subjects. "Is it not natural and necessary, under such different circumstances," he asked, "that a different degree of freedom in the use of the press should be contemplated? . . ." Earlier, in a debate in the House of Representatives, Madison had said: "If we advert to the nature of Republican Government, we shall find that the censorial power is in the people over the Government, and not in the Government over the people. . . ." Of the exercise of that power by the press, his Report said: "In every state, probably, in the Union, the press has exerted a freedom of canvassing the merits and measures of public men, of every description, which has not been confined to the strict limits of the common law. On this footing the freedom of the press has stood; on this foundation it yet stands. . . ." The right of free public discussion of the stewardship of public officials was thus, in Madison's view, a fundamental principle of the American form of government.

Although the Sedition Act was never tested in this Court,[1] the attack upon its validity has carried the day in the court of history. Fines levied in its prosecution were repaid by Act of Congress on the ground that it was unconstitutional. . . . Calhoun, reporting to the Senate on February 4, 1836, assumed that its invalidity was a matter "which no one now doubts. . . ." Jefferson, as President, pardoned those who had been convicted and sentenced under the Act and remitted their fines, stating: "I discharged every person under punishment or prosecution under the Sedition Law because I considered, and now consider, that law to be a nullity as abso-

---

[1] The Act expired by its terms in 1801.

lute and palpable as if Congress had ordered us to fall down and worship a golden image. . . ." The invalidity of the Act has also been assumed by Justices of this Court. . . . These views reflect a broad consensus that the Act, because of the restraint it imposed upon criticism of government and public officials, was inconsistent with the First Amendment.

There is no force in respondent's argument that the constitutional limitations implicit in the history of the Sedition Act apply only to Congress and not to the States. It is true that the First Amendment was originally addressed only to action by the Federal Government, and that Jefferson, for one, while denying the power of Congress "to controul the freedom of the press," recognized such a power in the States. . . . But this distinction was eliminated with the adoption of the Fourteenth Amendment and the application to the States of the First Amendment's restrictions. . . .

What a State may not constitutionally bring about by means of a criminal statute is likewise beyond the reach of its civil law of libel. The fear of damage awards under a rule such as that invoked by the Alabama courts here may be markedly more inhibiting than the fear of prosecution under a criminal statute. . . . Alabama, for example, has a criminal libel law which subjects to prosecution "any person who speaks, writes, or prints of and concerning another any accusation falsely and maliciously importing the commission by such person of a felony, or any other indictable offense involving moral turpitude," and which allows as punishment upon conviction a fine not exceeding $500 and a prison sentence of six months. . . . Presumably a person charged with violation of this statute enjoys ordinary criminal-law safeguards such as the requirements of an indictment and of proof beyond a reasonable doubt. These safeguards are not available to the defendant in a civil action. The judgment awarded in this case—without the need for any proof of actual pecuniary loss—was one thousand times greater than the maximum fine provided by the Alabama criminal statute, and one hundred times greater than that provided by the Sedition Act. And since there is no double-jeopardy limitation applicable to civil lawsuits, this is not the only judgment that may be awarded against petitioners for the same publication. Whether or not a newspaper can survive a succession of such judgments, the pall of fear and timidity imposed upon those who would give voice to public criticism is an atmosphere in which the First

Amendment freedoms cannot survive. Plainly the Alabama law of civil libel is "a form of regulation that creates hazards to protected freedoms markedly greater than those that attend reliance upon the criminal law. . . ."

The state rule of law is not saved by its allowance of the defense of truth. A defense for erroneous statements honestly made is no less essential here than was the requirement of proof of guilty knowledge which, in Smith v. California . . ., we held indispensable to a valid conviction of a bookseller for possessing obscene writings for sale. We said:

> For if the bookseller is criminally liable without knowledge of the contents, . . . he will tend to restrict the books he sells to those he has inspected; and thus the State will have imposed a restriction upon the distribution of constitutionally protected as well as obscene literature. . . . And the book-seller's burden would become the public's burden, for by restricting him the public's access to reading matter would be restricted. . . . [H]is timidity in the face of his absolute criminal liability, thus would tend to restrict the public's access to forms of the printed word which the State could not constitutionally suppress directly. The bookseller's selfcensorship, compelled by the State, would be a censorship affecting the whole public, hardly less virulent for being privately administered. Through it, the distribution of all books, both obscene and not obscene, would be impeded.

A rule compelling the critic of official conduct to guarantee the truth of all his factual assertions—and to do so on pain of libel judgments virtually unlimited in amount—leads to a comparable "self-censorship." Allowance of the defense of truth, with the burden of proving it on the defendant, does not mean that only false speech will be deterred. Even courts accepting this defense as an adequate safeguard have recognized the difficulties of adducing legal proofs that the alleged libel was true in all its factual particulars. . . . Under such a rule, would-be critics of official conduct may be deterred from voicing their criticism, even though it is believed to be true and even though it is in fact true, because of doubt whether it can be proved in court or fear of the expense of having to do so. They tend to make only statements which "steer far wider of the unlawful zone. . . ." The rule thus dampens the vigor and limits the variety of public debate. It is inconsistent with the First and Fourteenth Amendments.

The constitutional guarantees require, we think, a federal rule that prohibits a public official from recovering damages for a defamatory falsehood relating to his official conduct unless he proves that the statement was made with "actual malice"—that is, with knowledge that it was false or with reckless disregard of whether it was false or not. . . .

Reversed and remanded.

HARRY KALVEN

A New Look at the Central Meaning of the First Amendment

Harry Kalven is a professor of law at the University of Chicago Law School. In the selection reprinted below, he maintains that the opinion of the Court in the New York Times *case did much more than modify the law of libel. It suggested new approaches for interpreting the First Amendment and provided a fresh idiom for considering free speech problems. In his view, it appears to be a clear move toward interpreting freedom of speech as an absolute right.*

ON OCCASION THE SUPREME COURT hands down a decision in which past doctrine intersects present events in so complex a way as to be the despair of the commentator, not only because its portent is almost beyond prediction, but also because it opens so many avenues for inquiry. Just such a decision was *New York Times Co. v. Sullivan*[1] in which the Court unanimously held that a libel judgment rendered under Alabama law was violative of First Amendment principles and, therefore, of the Fourteenth Amendment.

. . . [M]y thesis is that the Court . . . wrote an opinion that may prove to be the best and most important it has ever produced in the

---

[1] 376 U.S. 254 (1964).

Reprinted from "The New York Times Case: A Note on the Central Meaning of the First Amendment," by Harry Kalven, Jr., *The Supreme Court Review* (1964), pp. 194–196, 204–213, 220–221, by permission of The University of Chicago Press. Copyright 1964 By the University of Chicago.

realm of freedom of speech. I would make it clear, however, that I am not so much predicting what the Court will do with the case as a precedent as I am suggesting that the opinion makes a notable shift in constitutional idiom and could provide a new start for consideration of free-speech problems. Implicit in this approach is a distinction between the history of legal ideas and precedent, at least at the constitutional level. Certainly the Court's ideas about freedom of speech have commanded as much attention and interest as its rulings. . . .

The exciting possibilities in the Court's opinion derive from its emphasis on seditious libel and the Sedition Act of 1798 as the key to the meaning of the First Amendment. My thesis is dependent on four propositions. First, that the importance of the free-speech provision of the Constitution rests on the rejection of seditious libel as an offense. Second, that constitutional history and the traditional analysis had relegated the concept of seditious libel to a curiously unimportant place, although the nagging question of the constitutionality of the Sedition Act of 1798 had never properly been put to rest. Third, that the special virtue of the *Times* opinion is its restoration of seditious libel to its essential role, thus suddenly and dramatically changing the idiom of free-speech analysis and resolving the question of the constitutionality of the Sedition Act. Finally, that the effect of the *Times* opinion is necessarily to discard or diminish in importance the clear-and-present-danger test, the balancing formula, the two-level speech theory of *Beauharnais* and *Roth,* and the two-tier theory of different effects of the First Amendment on federal and state action. If I am right, the *Times* case represents a happy revolution of free-speech doctrine. Or, to put the matter differently, analysis of free-speech issues should hereafter begin with the significant issue of seditious libel and defamation of government by its critics rather than with the sterile example of a man falsely yelling fire in a crowded theater.

My first proposition need not detain us long. The concept of seditious libel strikes at the very heart of democracy. Political freedom ends when government can use its powers and its courts to silence its critics. My point is not the tepid one that there should be leeway for criticism of the government. It is rather that defamation of the government is an impossible notion for a democracy. In brief, I suggest, that the presence or absence in the law of the concept of seditious libel defines the society. A society may or may not treat obscenity or contempt by publication as legal offenses without altering its basic nature. If, however, it makes seditious libel an offense, it is not a free society no matter what its other characteristics.

My second proposition, the denigration of the importance of seditious libel in establishing First Amendment principles, is more difficult to establish. Perhaps it is only the accident of the sequence in which the speech cases have come to the Court, combined with the fact that the Court never had the sedition laws before it, that leaves the impression of its disregard of seditious libel and its fascination with the clear-and-present-danger formula and balancing. Perhaps it is because we have not used functional categories in working out the theory of free speech. In any event, we do not start with the notion that seditious libel is clearly beyond the power of government and develop our ideas from that proposition.

Certainly, the logic of the clear-and-present-danger test does not foreclose the matter. It leaves the status of seditious libel in doubt. It does not suggest that severe criticism of government policy could never be sufficiently dangerous. Indeed, one might cite *Schenck, Debs,* and *Abrams* as three cases in which the Court itself reached the opposite conclusion.

Moreover, until its disposition by the *Times* case, the status of the Sedition Act of 1798 remained an open question. It has been a term of infamy in American usage, but sober judgments about its constitutionality have been few indeed. Many distinguished commentators—Corwin,[2] Hall,[3] and Carroll,[4] for example—regarded the Sedition Act as constitutional, and Story might also be numbered among them. Even Chafee, who makes a strong case for the unconstitutionality of the Act in the opening chapter of his classic, seems willing to leave the question unresolved. More recent researches by Crosskey and Levy have demonstrated how awkward a problem the Sedition Act presents. My point, for the moment, is not to choose the better view of the history of the First Amendment and the Sedition Act, but rather to call attention to the fact that for over 150 years it was not thought necessary to establish the status of the Act as a first step in getting to the meaning of the

[2] Corwin, *Freedom of Speech and Press under the First Amendment: A Resumé,* 30 YALE L. J. 48 (1920).

[3] Hall, *Free Speech in War Time,* 21 COLUM. L. REV. 526 (1921).

[4] Carroll, *Freedom of Speech and of the Press in the Federalist Period: The Sedition Act,* 18 MICH. L. REV. 615 (1920).

First Amendment. It was thus possible for the Espionage Act of
1917, as amended in 1918, to contain sections that oddly echoed
the idiom of seditious libel: "language intended to bring the form
of government of the United States . . . or the Constitution . . . or
the flag . . . or the uniform of the Army or Navy into contempt,
scorn, contumely, or disrepute." And it was possible for the Government solemnly to urge that the Sedition Act was constitutional in
its argument in the *Abrams* case in 1919.

Then there was the performance of the Court in 1952 in *Beauharnais v. Illinois,* where the majority, in an opinion by Mr. Justice
Frankfurter, upheld the constitutionality of a group-libel statute.
One might have expected that, in dealing with a question of the
application of defamation to comments about a public issue—the
alleged activities of Negroes moving into white neighborhoods,
the principal task of the Court would be to distinguish group
libel from seditious libel. Yet the majority opinion is virtually
silent on the point.

I turn, then, to the third proposition concerned with the meaning
of the Court's opinion in the *Times* case. I suggest that the critical
statement in Mr. Justice Brennan's opinion is: "If neither factual
error not defamatory content suffices to remove the constitutional
shield from criticism of official conduct, the combination of the
two elements is no less inadequate. This is the lesson to be drawn
from the great controversy over the Sedition Act of 1798, 1 Stat.
586, which first crystallized a national awareness of the central
meaning of the First Amendment. See Levy, Legacy of Suppression
(1960), at 258 *et seq.* . . ." There follows an extended discussion of
the "great controversy," with appropriate quotations from Madison
whose views the Court summarizes thus: "The right of free public
discussion of the stewardship of public officials was thus, in Madison's view, a fundamental principle of the American form of government."

The Court then, for the first time in its history and some 166
years after the enactment of the Sedition Act, turned squarely to
the issue of its constitutionality. The answer was that "the attack
upon its validity has carried the day in the court of history." The
opinion cited Jefferson, Calhoun, Holmes, Brandeis, Jackson, Douglas, Cooley, and Chafee and concluded: "These views reflect a
broad consensus that the Act, because of the restraint it imposed
upon criticism of government and public officials, was inconsistent
with the First Amendment."

The Court did not simply, in the face of an awkward history, definitively put to rest the status of the Sedition Act. More important, it found in the controversy over seditious libel the clue to "the central meaning of the First Amendment." The choice of language was unusually apt. The Amendment has a "central meaning" —a core of protection of speech without which democracy cannot function, without which, in Madison's phrase, "the censorial power" would be in the Government over the people and not "in the people over the Government." This is not the whole meaning of the Amendment. There are other freedoms protected by it. But at the center there is no doubt what speech is being protected and no doubt why it is being protected. The theory of the freedom of speech clause was put right side up for the first time.

Although the total structure of the opinion is not without its difficulties, it seems to me to convey, however imperfectly, the following crucial syllogism: The central meaning of the Amendment is that seditious libel cannot be made the subject of government sanction. The Alabama rule on fair comment is closely akin to making seditious libel an offense. The Alabama rule therefore violated the central meaning of the Amendment.

If the opinion can be read in this way, what emerges as of large importance is the generous sweep of the major premise and not the application of it to the point of defamation law involved in the *Times* case. The touchstone of the First Amendment has become the abolition of seditious libel and what that implies about the function of free speech on public issues in American democracy. The drama of the *Times* case then is that the Court, forced to extricate itself from the political impasse that was presented to it, did so by returning to the essence of the First Amendment to be found in its limitations on seditious libel. It gets to very high ground indeed.

There are two other portions of the opinion, already noted, that confirm the proposition that the Court is carried along by a momentum of insight about the democratic necessities for free speech. There is the analogy to *Barr v. Matteo* and the privilege of the high-ranking government executive. The rationale in *Barr* was that the threat of damage suits would dampen the ardor of the official for the performance of his duties. "Analogous considerations support the privilege for the citizen-critic of government. It is as much his duty to criticize as it is the official's duty to administer." It is now not only the citizen's privilege to criticize his government, it is his duty. At this point in its rhetoric and sweep, the opinion almost literally incorporated Alexander Meiklejohn's thesis that in a democracy the citizen as ruler is our most important public official.

Then there is the alternative ground for judgment concerned with the inadequate linking of the plaintiff to the language of the advertisement. If such connection is too easily made, all criticism of government policy, however impersonal, will carry implicit defamation of whatever officials were in charge of the policy attacked. Such a rule of construction, said Mr. Justice Brennan, "would sidestep this [constitutional] obstacle by transmuting criticism of government, however impersonal it may seem on its face, into personal criticism, and hence potential libel, of the officials of whom the government is composed. There is no legal alchemy by which a State may thus create the cause of action that would otherwise be denied. . . ." And then, to underscore the centrality of seditious libel for the First Amendment, Mr. Justice Brennan added: "Raising as it does the possibility that a good faith critic of government will be penalized for his criticism, the proposition relied on by the Alabama courts strikes at the very center of the constitutionally protected area of free expression."

When these three passages are taken together, it becomes evident that the Court was not simply uttering, as the Court is wont to do, the occasional sentence that reads felicitously even out of context. It was clearly being driven by a concern for the central meaning of the First Amendment.

The Court's confrontation of the relevance of truth to a constitutional doctrine of free speech, closely related as it is to the idea of seditious libel, requires further consideration. Here again Mr. Justice Brennan's observations are refreshing because they far transcend in importance the resolution of the specific issue before the Court.

The question may be asked: Does the constitutional protection of freedom of speech simply establish the right to utter the truth? History makes clear that this would be no inconsiderable freedom. Certainly there are various interesting limitations in contemporary law on the immunity of truth tellers. The critical question, however, is whether falsity must not also be protected. The classic defenses of freedom of speech have all suggested that the truth should not be used to discriminate between permissible and impermissible speech, at least at the level of ideas. More recently the point has been effectively put by Alexander Meiklejohn: "The vital point . . .

is that no suggestion of policy shall be denied a hearing because
it is on one side of the issue rather than another. . . . These conflicting views may be expressed, must be expressed, not because they
are valid, but because they are relevant."

For at least a generation it has been the prevailing notion that at
the level of doctrine and ideas the Constitution did not distinguish
between the true and the false. A short time ago, the proposition
was admirably summed up by Mr. Justice Stewart in the *Kingsley
Pictures* case which was concerned with a state ban on the movie
based on *Lady Chatterley's Lover:*

It is contended that the State's action was justified because the motion
picture attractively portrays a relationship which is contrary to the moral
standards, the religious precepts, and the legal code of its citizenry. This
argument misconceives what it is that the Constitution protects. Its guarantee is not confined to the expression of ideas that are conventional or
shared by a majority. It protects advocacy of the opinion that adultery may
sometimes be proper, no less than advocacy of socialism or the single tax.
And in the realm of ideas it protects expression which is eloquent no less
than that which is unconvincing.

What has been less clear was the vulnerability to legal discipline
of false statements of fact. And it was to this issue that Mr. Justice
Brennan spoke with such force in the opinion in the *Times* case.
False statements of fact, at least on public issues, are apparently to
be afforded constitutional protection. Two different rationales were
tendered in support of this proposition. There was stress on the
likelihood that errors of fact will be made. The Court, thus, approv-
ingly quoted from *Cantwell*'s behavioral dictum: "To persuade others
of his own point of view, the pleader, as we know, at times resorts
to exaggeration, to vilification of men who have been or are promi-
nent in church or state, and even to false statement." The Court
went on to state: ". . . erroneous statement is inevitable in free
debate, and . . . must be protected if the freedoms of expression
are to have the 'breathing space' that they 'need . . . to survive.' "
Once again we are reminded that the national commitment is to
debate on public issues that is "uninhibited, robust, and wide open."

The Court is also moved, however, by the difficulty of proving
truth in these matters, and of putting the speaker to the risk of
proof before fallible judges, juries, or administrative officials. In
dealing with this proposition, the Court put together *Smith v. California* and *Speiser v. Randall* to suggest a new category of invalid

regulations: laws that tend to inhibit freedom of speech by generating a kind of "self-censorship." Thus, the bookseller in *Smith,* if left under so loose a requirement of scienter of obscenity, would tend to restrict the books he sells to those he has inspected. The law would then set off a chain reaction of self-censorship "affecting the whole public, hardly less virulent for being privately administered." And the citizen seeking tax exemption in *Speiser,* confronted with the loyalty test there involved which left the burden of proof on the applicant, would become comparably reticent. "The man who knows that he must bring forth proof and persuade another of the lawfulness of his conduct necessarily must steer far wider of the unlawful zone than if the State must bear these burdens." So too in the *Times* case, the "critic of official conduct" would be deterred from uttering what was in fact true "because of doubt whether it can be proved in court or fear of the expense of having to do so." Thus the special vice of such a law is that it introduces a self-censorship that invades the zone of permissible and lawful speech. From these three cases, all written by Mr. Justice Brennan, emerges a fascinating and promising judicial utilization of psychology.

It must be recognized, of course, that a reason implicit in the breadth of the protection afforded speech is due to the judicial recognition of its own incapacity to make nice discriminations. It reflects a strategy that requires that speech be overprotected in order to assure that it is not underprotected. In any event, the *Times* opinion is as great a contribution to the issue of the relevance of truth to protected speech as it is to the issue of the relevance of the doctrine of seditious libel. . . .

Conclusion

We get a sense of difference between a legal theory of freedom of speech and a philosophic theory as we trace the career of seditious libel from seventeenth-century England through Fox's Libel Act through the Sedition Act to the *Times* case. It is one thing to assert that a vigorous criticism of the government must be permitted. It is another to choose among the calibrations of freedom that legal institutions and procedures can provide. Initially the great issue about seditious libel was whether judge or jury would have the final say as to what was defamatory of the government. The effect of Fox's Libel Act was simply to shift control from the judges to the juries, from the government and its judges to the people themselves. Then it became important to establish truth as a defense. And, finally, in the *Times* case the critical area involves the degree of privilege to be afforded statements that are not true. We are reminded not only of how much more complex the legal debate over freedom of speech or over seditious libel can be, but again of the arresting problem how much freedom of speech in a legal system must depend on law's conscious distrust of its own processes to make needed discriminations.

The closing question, of course, is whether the treatment of seditious libel as the key concept for development of appropriate constitutional doctrine will prove germinal. It is not easy to predict what the Court will see in the *Times* opinion as the years roll by. It may regard the opinion as covering simply one pocket of cases, those dealing with libel of public officials, and not destructive of the earlier notions that are inconsistent only with the larger reading of the Court's action. But the invitation to follow a dialectic progression from public official to government policy to public policy to matters in the public domain, like art, seems to me to be overwhelming. If the Court accepts the invitation, it will slowly work out for itself the theory of free speech that Alexander Meiklejohn has been offering us for some fifteen years now.

JUDGE HAROLD R. MEDINA

Students Have Constitutional Rights Too

Harold R. Medina is a judge for the United States Court of Appeals, Second Circuit; he presided at the trial of the 11 top Communists in 1949. In 1965, a number of students staged a protest against the war in Vietnam at the local office of the draft board in Ann Arbor, Michigan. Subsequently, two students involved in that protest had their Selective Service classifications

Judge Harold R. Medina speaking for the U. S. Court of Appeals, 2nd Circuit, in *Wolff and Shortt v. The Selective Service Local Boards No. 16 and 66 and Col. Paul Akst, Director of the New York City Headquarters, Selective Service System,* 1967. Some case citations omitted.

changed from II-S to I-A. The students contended that they were being punished for exercising their constitutional right to express their views on national policy and sought an injunction from a federal district court to bar the reclassification. The lower court denied relief; however, in the opinion reprinted below, Judge Medina, speaking for the Court of Appeals, reversed the lower court and upheld the free speech claim of the students. He pointed out, as did Justice Brennan in the Times *case, that the mere* threat *of sanctions may have the effect of destroying First Amendment rights as much as if the sanctions were actually applied.*

PETER WOLFF AND RICHARD SHORTT, registrants of Selective Service Boards No. 66 in Queens County and No. 16 in New York County were classified II-S because of their status as full-time students at the University of Michigan. On October 15, 1965 these students and others participated in a demonstration to protest American involvement in Vietnam, at the offices of a Selective Service local board in Ann Arbor, Michigan. At the request of the New York City Director of Selective Service the local boards reclassified the two students I-A. The request was based upon the assertion that by participating in the demonstration the students became "delinquents" by reason of their alleged violation of Section 12(a) of the Universal Military Training and Service Act. Claiming that the local boards acted wholly without jurisdiction and in violation of their First Amendment rights of free speech and assembly and of their Sixth Amendment rights as well, Wolff and Shortt brought this action against the local boards and the Director to bring about a return of their student deferments. On motion, based upon the allegations appearing on the face of the complaint, Judge McLean dismissed the action for lack of "a justiciable controversy" and Wolff and Shortt appeal.

We disagree. The two local boards did act without jurisdiction, the record shows that attempts to secure relief within the Selective Service System would be futile, and the threat to First Amendment rights is of such immediate and irreparable consequence not simply to these students but to others as to require prompt action by the courts to avoid an erosion of these precious constitutional rights. Under this combination of circumstances an injunction could properly issue. . . .

Irrespective of the existence of the power to do so, the courts, and particularly this Court, have been extremely reluctant to bring any phase of the operation of the Selective Service System under judicial scrutiny. The very nature of the Service demands that it operate with maximum efficiency, unimpeded by external interference. Only the most weighty consideration could induce us to depart from this long standing policy. But of all constitutional rights, the freedoms of speech and of assembly are the most perishable, yet the most vital to the preservation of American democracy. Historically, these preferred and paramount rights have continually come under attack from the best intentioned sources. And once the erosion of these rights is permitted to begin, it is exceedingly difficult to halt and the intervening damage may be irreparable. Here it is the free expression of views on issues of critical current national importance that is jeopardized. On such topics perhaps more than any other, it is imperative that the public debate be full and that each segment of our society be permitted freely to express its views. Thus the allegations of the complaint in this case that the draft boards have unlawfully suppressed criticism must take precedence over the policy of non-intervention in the affairs of the Selective Service. . . .

The Government further argues that this case is not ripe for adjudication because appellants have failed to exhaust their administrative remedies and because they cannot demonstrate irreparable injury. The courts ordinarily will not adjudicate a matter which may become moot through subsequent action by the executive. Nor will the courts hear a cause when the action complained of has not caused or is not certain to cause injury to the complaining party. In other words, a federal court cannot render an advisory opinion.

Thus in the usual run of Selective Service cases, the registrant must wait until he receives an induction order, and has either obeyed it or is prosecuted for refusing to obey it, before the courts may review his classification. This is so because, in nearly all cases, it is service in the armed forces itself, and not the mere classification, that constitutes the alleged injury. Thus, should it develop that for independent reasons such as physical disability the registrant is not actually wanted by the armed forces, he will never have sustained a legally redressible injury. Perhaps it is true that a mere adverse classification will cause a disarray of plans and emotional upset but this is an acceptable price to pay for the efficient functioning of the Selective Service and it has been universally held that such injury is not sufficient to entitle a registrant to pre-induction order relief.

But, while the general run of cases do not present a justiciable controversy, it does not follow that no case can. Here it is not relevant whether or not appellants will ever be inducted. The effect of the reclassification itself is immediately to curtail the exercise of First Amendment rights, for there can be no doubt that the threat of receiving a I-A classification upon voicing dissent from our national policies has an immediate impact on the behavior of appellants and others similarly situated.

It has been held repeatedly that the mere threat of the imposition of unconstitutional sanctions will cause immediate and irreparable injury to the free exercise of rights as fragile and sensitive to suppression as the freedoms of speech and assembly and the right to vote. Since it is the mere threat of unconstitutional sanctions which precipitates the injury, the courts must intervene at once to vindicate the threatened liberties.

Dombrowski v. *Pfister,* 380 U. S. 479 (1965), is very much in point. There a civil rights organization sought an injunction against various state officials against the threatened enforcement of a Subversives Control Law. It was alleged that the prosecution was being conducted without any real expectation of success and was in fact a deliberate harassment of the plaintiff. A three-judge District Court dismissed the complaint on the ground that there had been no showing of irreparable injury to federal rights and that the case was a proper one for abstention. Quite similarly to our case, the Supreme Court allowed that the inconveniences which normally accompany a prosecution were insufficient to invoke federal court intervention and that the rights of the appellants could ultimately be vindicated through the normal procedures. Nevertheless, the Court reversed the District Court and held, first, that irreparable injury had been alleged and, second, that abstention was not appropriate. Regarding the first point, the Court said:

[T]he allegations in this complaint depict a situation in which defense of the State's criminal prosecution will not assure adequate vindication of constitutional rights. They suggest that a substantial loss or impairment of freedoms of expression will occur if appellants must await the state court's disposition and ultimate review in this Court of any adverse determination. These allegations, if true, clearly show irreparable injury.

Here the injury caused by the threatened impairment of appellants' constitutional rights is magnified by the uncertainty as to the standard which the Service has applied. As there is no statute or regulation to guide the local boards, the registrant cannot know whether sit-ins alone will be deemed a basis for reclassification or whether sidewalk demonstrations or even more remote conduct are to be included.

Where basic constitutional rights are imperiled, the courts have not required a series of injured parties to litigate the permissible scope of the statute or administrative interpretation but have nullified the unconstitutional action and required the Government to start in the first instance with a statute or interpretation that will not so overhang free expression that the legitimate exercise of constitutionally protected rights is suppressed. . . . In our case intervention is especially appropriate because for reasons independent of the First Amendment the entire course of conduct of the appellee boards is illegal and cannot be saved by any amount of narrowing construction. . . .

Furthermore, the narrow facts presented on this appeal show clearly that no purpose would be served by relegating appellants to their administrative remedies.

Appellants were part of a larger group of demonstrators. Some of appellants' companions were similarly reclassified I-A and have completed their appeals within the administration. The national appeal board has concluded unanimously that the reclassifications were valid and, further, the National Director of the Selective Service has stated repeatedly that the reclassifications were proper. There are no facts which have been brought to our attention which would lead to a contrary result in appellants' case and we are most reluctant in a case of this importance to require appellants to proceed along the same futile path that others have trod before.

When there is nothing to be gained from the exhaustion of administrative remedies and the harm from the continued existence of the administrative ruling is great, the courts have not been reluctant to discard this doctrine.

We are well aware that many reported cases contain language, . . . relied upon below, to the general effect that the review of classification orders is possible only in criminal proceedings or on habeas corpus petitions. But we have discovered no case which contained the allegation that the classification by the board had the immediate effect of depriving the registrant of his First Amendment rights. Nor, in fact, have we discovered any case in which the board exceeded its jurisdiction as clearly as did the appellee boards in this case.

THE SELECTIVE SERVICE
RECLASSIFICATION CONTROVERSY

CHARLES W. SCHIESSER AND
DANIEL H. BENSON

The Case for Reclassifying Student Protesters

Major Charles W. Schiesser and Captain Daniel H. Benson are members of the staff of the Judge Advocate General, United States Army. They answer criticism of some draft boards that reclassified students who participated in demonstrations against the Vietnam war. The authors examine the duties of draft boards and explain how the reclassification system works, and they contend that it is incorrect to say that reclassified students are being "punished" for their conduct.

ONE OF THE MOST SIGNIFICANT ASPECTS of the Selective Service System is the authority given to local Selective Service boards. Local boards, under appropriate rules and regulations prescribed by the President, have the power within their respective jurisdictions to hear and determine, subject to the right of appeal, all questions or

From Charles W. Schiesser and Daniel H. Benson, "The Legality of Reclassification of Selective Service Registrants," *American Bar Association Journal* (February, 1967), Vol. 53, pp. 149–153. Reprinted by permission of the *American Bar Association Journal.*

claims with respect to inclusion for or exemption or deferment from training and service. The local board has the authority and duty to make classification and reclassification determinations as to each registrant. Substantial controversy has arisen recently concerning the exercise of this classification and reclassification power.

It is the local board's responsibility to decide the class into which each registrant shall be placed, and in making that determination the board must consider each registrant as available for military training and service until such time as his eligibility for determent or exemption is clearly established to the satisfaction of the board. Thus, a deferment—even a student deferment—is not a matter of right but is a matter of legislative grace, and the burden is upon the registrant to show that he should not be deemed available for immediate military service. In reaching their decisions, the local boards are selecting a large segment of the nation's military personnel, and they must act for the benefit of the national welfare rather than primarily from the viewpoint of an individual registrant's personal interest or preference. These factors are often submerged in much of the current discussion and debate about classification and reclassification of registrants.

Classification is an essential step in the process of induction, and unless an appeal is taken to a Selective Service appeal board, the local board's decision on a registrant's claim for deferment is final. It is again emphasized that the burden is upon the registrant to establish his eligibility for deferment or exemption from military training and service to the satisfaction of the local board, and the courts cannot review the correctness of a board's action if there is any evidence or "basis in fact" to support the decision of the board unless it is shown that the board's action was arbitrary and capricious, based on bias or prejudice, or that the registrant was denied a procedural right and such denial was actually prejudicial to his substantial rights. Judicial review may be granted or withheld, as Congress sees fit, and jurisdiction to review the findings of local boards is not conferred upon the courts by the act or any other statute. Consequently, the scope of judicial review into the administrative proceedings of the Selective Service System is very limited— "the range of review is the narrowest known to the law"—and the courts do not sit as "super draft boards."

It is within the context of these rules and holdings that the entire classification process must be evaluated if an adequate understanding of the issues involved is to be obtained. . . .

There is perhaps more misunderstanding about the matter of reclassification than any other subject concerning the operations of the local boards. It is being charged by various groups and individuals that some Selective Service boards have "punished" nonconformist registrants, "convicted" them without benefit of a fair trial and "sentenced" them to induction and service in the Armed Forces for their participation in demonstrations and related antiwar activities. It is true that a local board is entitled (and is under a positive duty) to respond to information coming to its attention regarding the conduct of any of its registrants. It is also true that the board's response may ultimately result in induction, after reclassification, of a registrant. And it is true that, as outlined briefly above, the local boards will not duplicate or even attempt to duplicate trial court procedures in responding to information regarding their registrants. But given all of these things, it does not follow that the local boards have acted either unfairly or unconstitutionally.

A local board of the Selective Service System is not empowered to adjudicate fine points of constitutional law, for that is no part of its legitimate function. Nor is a local board engaged in the business of passing upon the most appropriate methods of protest to be utilized by students who are disturbed about the prospect of having to help in defending the nation. It is the task of the local board to raise manpower for a significant part of our Armed Forces by administering the statutes that require all eligible male citizens to render military service.

In accomplishing its proper business, the local board may reevaluate whether its prior determinations are still valid, as to each and every registrant, in light of any and all new or changed circumstances or conditions. In the process, the local board will sometimes determine that a prior classification was in error or is no longer valid for a particular registrant. The local board has a duty to reclassify a registrant who has been given a deferment when that registrant fails to carry his burden of establishing to the continuing satisfaction of the board that his temporary deferment is in the best interests of the nation.

Of course, in the usual situation, a local board will reopen a case and reclassify a registrant only when he submits evidence of changed circumstances and files a written request for a reopening of his classification. But the local board may determine whether to reopen and reclassify on its own motion, and it may do so even in the absence of new evidence, unless an order to report for induction has been issued.

It is expected that litigation will arise in some volume from the local boards' reclassification of various "student demonstrators." On the basis of the prior case holdings, it appears likely that the courts will sustain the reclassifications if the sole basis for the attack is that the student registrant in question had a "constitutional right to protest." Surely no one would question the right of a citizen freely to express his views, but what is involved in a local board reclassification proceeding is the *privilege* (not the *right*) of an individual who is under a statutory duty to render military service to continue to postpone that duty while he seeks to complete a part or all of his education.

An enormous variety of subjective factors must be considered and weighed by the local board as it seeks to determine whether the national interest would best be served by the particular student's continuing deferment. Not the least of these factors is the extent to which the student registrant's conduct indicates that he is sincere in his desire for completion of his education, willing to abide by the laws of his city, state and nation while in a student status, and actually making progress in a satisfactory manner toward completion of his education. Deans of colleges and universities certainly take into account a student's conduct, on and off campus, in determining whether the student should continue his course of study; it is no less reasonable for local boards of the Selective Service System to do the same.

It may be unfortunate if the student registrant happens to disagree, in a particular situation, with the standards of the members of his local board concerning the kind of conduct that is acceptable as indicating satisfactory progress in his education and probable success in completing it, yet the burden of proof, first, last and always, is on the student registrant. There is no burden of proof at all on the board. Consequently, as between the student registrant and the board, the burden of establishing a pattern of conduct indicative of probable academic success and resulting probable benefit to the nation if military service is further deferred is in the final analysis on the student registrant alone, not on the local board.

The authors are aware of no instance in which any registrant has been reclassified merely because of his expressed disagreement with either the principles of the Selective Service System generally, or

national foreign policy specifically, where his expressions of disagreement may reasonably be considered as an exercise of free
speech. This includes the distribution of leaflets, the carrying of
placards, picketing, speaking and like forms of communication.

To the best of the authors' knowledge, it is only when these
activities have been carried on in such a manner as actually to interfere with the operations of the Selective Service System directly that
reclassification has occurred. For example, the "student demonstrators" in the widely publicized cases at Ann Arbor, Michigan, in
October of 1965 crowded into the public area of a local board office
and then sat or stood for almost an entire afternoon while engaging
in singing, chanting, hand clapping, shouting, stomping and loud
talking, which made it impossible for the local board personnel to
carry on their work and hindered other registrants in the transaction
of legitimate business with the local board. In view of this interference with the operations of the local board, many of the boards with
which those Michigan "student demonstrators" are registered gave
further consideration to whether the continued deferment of such
students was in the best interest of the nation. In so doing, the local
boards recognized the difference between unlawful interference with
the operations of the Selective Service System and lawful, peaceful
protest constituting the exercise of free speech. The former led to
reclassification; the latter did not.

It is a hard fact that a student registrant must accept the risk of
the natural and probable consequences of his acts of "protest" or
"demonstration" as embodied in the thinking of the members of his
local Selective Service board when they review his conduct in the
light of their statutory duty to determine whether deferment should
be continued. If the local board determines that the student registrant's deferment is no longer in the best interests of the nation,
then deferment will be terminated and the student registrant will
have to embark upon the fulfillment of his statutory obligation to
render military service.

The classification and reclassification procedures do not constitute
"trial", "conviction" or "punishment" in any sense. If classification
or reclassification brings about a result that is viewed by the student
registrant as punishment, that is a private, subjective matter. Undoubtedly there will always be some individuals and groups who
regard any military service on behalf of their country as a punishment of sorts, but private views are not at issue. The issue is whether

the local boards are in any way violating the laws or the Constitution solely by discretionary reclassification of student registrants. It is submitted that they are not.

NEGRO DEMONSTRATORS AND THE FIRST AMENDMENT

MR. JUSTICE POTTER STEWART

Peaceful Protest at Capitol Building: Upheld

Potter Stewart was appointed to the U.S. Supreme Court in 1958 by President Eisenhower. In 1963, the Court dealt with the Edwards v. South Carolina *case, in which the basic question was whether the police were justified in arresting Negro students who were peacefully demonstrating on the state capitol grounds. The authorities maintained that they acted because of the threat of violence. The protest had attracted a crowd of 200 to 300 people, and there had been previous incidents of racial conflict in the State. The Supreme Court held that under the circumstances the arrests violated First Amendment rights. Undoubtedly the case for the police would have been more persuasive if there had been threats or actual violence and they had diligently tried to protect the peaceful demonstration before taking the final drastic action. Of course, one of the unarticulated questions running through this case is whether the police acted in good faith or whether they really objected to the fact that Negroes were challenging the establishment.*

Justice Potter Stewart in *Edwards v. South Carolina,* 372 U. S. 229 (1963). Case citations omitted.

THE PETITIONERS, 187 IN NUMBER, were convicted in a magistrate's court in Columbia, South Carolina, of the common-law crime of breach of the peace. . . .

There was no substantial conflict in the trial evidence. Late in the morning of March 2, 1961, the petitioners, high school and college students of the Negro race, met at the Zion Baptist Church in Columbia. From there, at about noon, they walked in separate groups of about 15 to the South Carolina State House grounds, an area of two city blocks open to the general public. Their purpose was "to submit a protest to the citizens of South Carolina, along with the Legislative Bodies of South Carolina, our feelings and our dissatisfaction with the present condition of discriminatory actions against Negroes, in general, and to let them know that we were dissatisfied and that we would like for the laws which prohibited Negro privileges in this State to be removed."

Already on the State House grounds when the petitioners arrived were 30 or more law enforcement officers, who had advance knowledge that the petitioners were coming. Each group of petitioners entered the grounds through a driveway and parking area known in the record as the "horseshoe." As they entered, they were told by the law enforcement officials that "they had a right, as a citizen, to go through the State House grounds, as any other citizen has, as long as they were peaceful." During the next half hour or 45 minutes, the petitioners, in the same small groups, walked single file or two abreast in an orderly way through the grounds, each group carrying placards bearing such messages as "I am proud to be a Negro," and "Down with segregation."

During this time a crowd of some 200 to 300 onlookers had collected in the horseshoe area and on the adjacent sidewalks. There was no evidence to suggest that these onlookers were anything but curious, and no evidence at all of any threatening remarks, hostile gestures, or offensive language on the part of any member of the crowd. The City Manager testified that he recognized some of the onlookers, whom he did not identify, as "possible trouble makers," but his subsequent testimony made clear that nobody among the crowd actually caused or threatened any trouble. There was no obstruction of pedestrian or vehicular traffic within the State House grounds. No vehicle was prevented from entering or leaving the horseshoe area. Although vehicular traffic at a nearby street intersection was slowed down somewhat, an officer was dispatched to keep traffic moving. There were a number of bystanders on the public sidewalks adjacent to the State House grounds, but they all moved on when asked to do so, and there was no impediment of pedestrian traffic. Police protection at the scene was at all times sufficient to meet any foreseeable possibility of disorder.

In the situation and under the circumstances thus described, the police authorities advised the petitioners that they would be arrested if they did not disperse within 15 minutes. Instead of dispersing, the petitioners engaged in what the City Manager described as "boisterous," "loud," and "flamboyant" conduct, which, as his later testimony made clear, consisted of listening to a "religious harangue" by one of their leaders, and loudly singing "The Star Spangled Banner" and other patriotic and religious songs, while stamping their feet and clapping their hands. After 15 minutes had passed, the police arrested the petitioners and marched them off to jail.

Upon this evidence the state trial court convicted the petitioners of breach of the peace, and imposed sentences ranging from a $10 fine or five days in jail, to a $100 fine or 30 days in jail. In affirming the judgments, the Supreme Court of South Carolina said that under the law of that State the offense of breach of the peace "is not susceptible of exact definition," but that the "general definition of the offense" is as follows:

"In general terms, a breach of the peace is a violation of public order, a disturbance of the public tranquility, by any act or conduct inciting to violence . . . , it includes any violation of any law enacted to preserve peace and good order. It may consist of an act of violence or an act likely to produce violence. It is not necessary that the peace be actually broken to lay the foundation for a prosecution for this offense. If what is done is unjustifiable and unlawful, tending with sufficient directness to break the peace, no more is required. Nor is actual personal violence an essential element in the offense. . . .

"By 'peace,' as used in the law in this connection, is meant the tranquility enjoyed by citizens of a municipality or community where good order reigns among its members, which is the natural right of all persons in political society." . . .

The petitioners contend that there was a complete absence of any evidence of the commission of this offense, and that they were thus denied one of the most basic elements of due process of law. . . . Whatever the merits of this contention, we need not pass upon it in the present case. The state courts have held that the petitioners' conduct constituted breach of the peace under state law, and we may accept their decision as binding upon us to that extent. But it nevertheless remains our duty in a case such as this to make an independent examination of the whole record. . . . And it is clear to us that in arresting, convicting, and punishing the petitioners under the circumstances disclosed by this record, South Carolina infringed the petitioners' constitutionally protected rights of free speech, free assembly, and freedom to petition for redress of their grievances.

It has long been established that these First Amendment freedoms are protected by the Fourteenth Amendment from invasion by the States. . . . The circumstances in this case reflect an exercise of these basic constitutional rights in their most pristine and classic form. The petitioners felt aggrieved by laws of South Carolina which allegedly "prohibited Negro privileges in this State." They peaceably assembled at the site of the State Government and there peaceably expressed their grievances "to the citizens of South Carolina, along with the Legislative Bodies of South Carolina." Not until they were told by police officials that they must disperse on pain of arrest did they do more. Even then, they but sang patriotic and religious songs after one of their leaders had delivered a "religious harangue." There was no violence or threat of violence on their part, or on the part of any member of the crowd watching them. Police protection was "ample."

This, therefore, was a far cry from the situation in Feiner v New York. . . . where two policemen were faced with a crowd which was "pushing, shoving, and milling around," . . . where at least one member of the crowd "threatened violence if the police did not act," . . . where "the crowd was pressing closer around petitioner and the officer," . . . and where "the speaker passes the bounds of argument or persuasion and undertakes incitement to riot." . . . And the record is barren of any evidence of "fighting words." . . .

We do not review in this case criminal convictions resulting from the even-handed application of a precise and narrowly drawn regulatory statute evincing a legislative judgment that certain specific conduct be limited or proscribed. If, for example, the petitioners had been convicted upon evidence that they had violated a law regulating traffic, or had disobeyed a law reasonably limiting the periods during which the State House grounds were open to the public, this would be a different case. . . . These petitioners were convicted of an offense so generalized as to be, in the words of the South Carolina Supreme Court, "not susceptible of exact definition." And they were convicted upon evidence which showed no more than that the opinions which they were peaceably expressing were sufficiently opposed to the views of the majority of the community to attract a crowd and necessitate police protection.

The Fourteenth Amendment does not permit a State to make criminal the peaceful expression of unpopular views. "[A] function of free speech under our system of government is to invite dispute. It may indeed best serve its high purpose when it induces a condition of unrest, creates dissatisfaction with conditions as they are, or even stirs people to anger. Speech is often provocative and challenging. It may strike at prejudices and preconceptions and have profound unsettling effects as it presses for acceptance of an idea. That is why freedom of speech, . . . is . . . protected against censorship or punishment, unless shown likely to produce a clear and present danger of a serious substantive evil that rises far above public inconvenience, annoyance, or unrest. . . . There is no room under our Constitution for a more restrictive view. For the alternative would lead to standardization of ideas either by legislatures, courts, or dominant political or community groups." . . . As in the Terminiello Case, the courts of South Carolina have defined a criminal offense so as to permit conviction of the petitioners if their speech "stirred people to anger, invited public dispute, or brought about a condition of unrest. A conviction resting on any of those grounds may not stand." . . .

As Chief Justice Hughes wrote in Stromberg v California, "The maintenance of the opportunity for free political discussion to the end that government may be responsive to the will of the people and that changes may be obtained by lawful means, an opportunity essential to the security of the Republic, is a fundamental principle of our constitutional system. A statute which upon its face, and as authoritatively construed, is so vague and indefinite as to permit the punishment of the fair use of this opportunity is repugnant to the guaranty of liberty contained in the Fourteenth Amendment." . . .

For these reasons we conclude that these criminal convictions cannot stand.

Reversed.

MR. JUSTICE HUGO L. BLACK

Peaceful Protest at the County Jail: Condemned

In Adderley v. Florida *(1966), a closely divided Supreme Court upheld the conviction of Negro students who had demonstrated at a county jail. According to Justice Black, the place of the demonstration and the fact that Florida had a specific statute to cover the incident were factors that distinguished this case from the South Carolina controversy. But were these really significant distinctions? Justice Douglas and three other dissenters did not think so.*

Opinion of The Court

MR. JUSTICE BLACK DELIVERED the opinion of the Court.

Petitioners, Harriett Louise Adderley and 31 other persons, were convicted by a jury in a joint trial in the County Judge's Court of Leon County, Florida, on a charge of "trespass with a malicious and mischievous intent" upon the premises of the county jail contrary to § 821.18 of the Florida statutes set out below.[1] . . . Disturbed and upset by the arrest of their schoolmates the day before, a large number of Florida A. & M. students assembled on the school grounds and decided to march down to the county jail. Some apparently wanted to get themselves put in jail too, along with the students already there. A group of around 200 marched from the school and arrived at the jail singing and clapping. They went directly to the jail door entrance where they were met by a deputy sheriff, evidently surprised by their arrival. He asked them to move back, claiming they were blocking the entrance to the jail and fearing that they might attempt to enter the jail. They moved back part

[1] "Every trespass upon property of another, committed with a malicious and mischievous intent, the punishment of which is not specially provided for, shall be punished by imprisonment not exceeding three months, or by fine not exceeding one hundred dollars." Fla Stat § 821.18 (1965).

Justice Hugo L. Black speaking for the majority in *Adderley v. Florida* 385 U.S. 39 (1966) Case citations omitted.

of the way, where they stood or sat, singing, clapping and dancing, on the jail driveway and on an adjacent grassy area upon the jail premises. This particular jail entrance and driveway were not normally used by the public, but by the sheriff's department for transporting prisoners to and from the courts several blocks away and by commercial concerns for servicing the jail. Even after their partial retreat, the demonstrators continued to block vehicular passage over this driveway up to the entrance of the jail. Someone called the sheriff who was at the moment apparently conferring with one of the state court judges about incidents connected with prior arrests for demonstrations. When the sheriff returned to the jail, he immediately inquired if all was safe inside the jail and was told it was. He then engaged in a conversation with two of the leaders. He told them that they were trespassing upon jail property and that he would give them 10 minutes to leave or he would arrest them. Neither of the leaders did anything to disperse the crowd, and one of them told the sheriff that they wanted to get arrested. A local minister talked with some of the demonstrators and told them not to enter the jail, because they could not arrest themselves, but just to remain where they were. After about 10 minutes, the sheriff, in a voice loud enough to be heard by all, told the demonstrators that he was the legal custodian of the jail and its premises, that they were trespassing on county property in violation of the law, that they should all leave forthwith or he would arrest them, and that if they attempted to resist arrest, he would charge them with that as a separate offense. Some of the group then left. Others, including all petitioners, did not leave. Some of them sat down. In a few minutes, realizing that the remaining demonstrators had no intention of leaving, the sheriff ordered his deputies to surround those remaining on jail premises and placed them, 107 demonstrators, under arrest. The sheriff unequivocally testified that he did not arrest any person other than those who were on the jail premises. Of the three petitioners testifying, two insisted that they were arrested before they had a chance to leave, had they wanted to, and one testified that she did not intend to leave. The sheriff again explicitly testified that he did not arrest any person who was attempting to leave.

Under the foregoing testimony the jury was authorized to find that the State had proven every essential element of the crime, as it was defined by the court. That interpretation is, of course, binding on us, leaving only the question of whether conviction of the state offense, thus defined, unconstitutionally deprives petitioners of their rights to freedom of speech, press, assembly or petition. We hold it does not. The sheriff, as jail custodian, had power, as the state courts have here held, to direct that this large crowd of people get off the grounds. There is not a shred of evidence in this record that this power was exercised, or that its exercise was sanctioned by the lower courts, because the sheriff objected to what was being sung or said by the demonstrators or because he disagreed with the objectives of their protest. The record reveals that he objected only to their presence on that part of the jail grounds reserved for jail uses. There is no evidence at all that on any other occasion had similarly large groups of the public been permitted to gather on this portion of the jail grounds for any purpose. Nothing in the Constitution of the United States prevents Florida from even-handed enforcement of its general trespass statute against those refusing to obey the sheriff's order to remove themselves from what amounted to the curtilage of the jailhouse. The State, no less than a private owner of property, has power to preserve the property under its control for the use to which it is lawfully dedicated. For this reason there is no merit to the petitioners' argument that they had a constitutional right to stay on the property, over the jail custodian's objections, because this "area chosen for the peaceful civil rights demonstration was not only 'reasonable' but also particularly appropriate. . . ." Such an argument has as its major unarticulated premise the assumption that people who want to propagandize protests or views have a constitutional right to do so whenever and however and wherever they please. That concept of constitutional law was vigorously and forthrightfully rejected in two of the cases petitioners rely on. . . . We reject it again. The United States Constitution does not forbid a State to control the use of its own property for its own lawful nondiscriminatory purpose.

These judgments are affirmed.

Separate Opinion

Mr. Justice Douglas, with whom The Chief Justice, Mr. Justice Brennan, and Mr. Justice Fortas concur, dissenting.

The First Amendment . . . provides that "Congress shall make no law respecting . . . the right of the people peaceably to assemble, and to petition the government for a redress of grievances." These rights, along with religion, speech, and press, are preferred rights of the Constitution, made so by reason of that explicit guarantee and what Edmond Cahn in Confronting Injustice (1966) referred to as "The Firstness of the First Amendment." With all respect, therefore, the Court errs in treating the case as if it were an ordinary trespass case or an ordinary picketing case.

The jailhouse, like an executive mansion, a legislative chamber, a courthouse, or the statehouse itself (Edwards v South Carolina, supra) is one of the seats of government whether it be the Tower of London, the Bastille, or a small county jail. And when it houses political prisoners or those whom many think are unjustly held, it is an obvious center for protest. The right to petition for the redress of grievances has an ancient history and is not limited to writing a letter or sending a telegram to a congressman; it is not confined to appearing before the local city council, or writing letters to the President or Governor or Mayor. . . . Conventional methods of petitioning may be, and often have been, shut off to large groups of our citizens. Legislators may turn deaf ears; formal complaints may be routed endlessly through a bureaucratic maze; courts may let the wheels of justice grind very slowly. Those who do not control television and radio, those who cannot afford to advertise in newspapers or circulate elaborate pamphlets may have only a more limited type of access to public officials. Their methods should not be condemned as tactics of obstruction and harassment as long as the assembly and petition are peaceable, as these were.

There is no question that petitioners had as their purpose a protest against the arrest of Florida A. & M. students for trying to integrate public theatres. The sheriff's testimony indicates that he well understood the purpose of the rally. The petitioners who testified unequivocally stated that the group was protesting the arrests, and state and local policies of segregation, including segregation of the jail. This testimony was not contradicted or even questioned. The fact that no one gave a formal speech, that no elaborate handbills were distributed, and that the group was not laden with signs would seem to be immaterial. Such methods are not the sine qua non of petitioning for the redress of grievances. The group did sing "freedom" songs. And history shows that a song can be a powerful tool of protest. . . . There was no violence; no threats of violence; no attempted jail break; no storming of a prison; no plan or plot to do anything but protest. The evidence is uncontradicted that the petitioners' conduct did not upset the jailhouse routine; things went on as they normally would. None of the group entered the jail. Indeed, they moved back from the entrance as they were instructed. There was no shoving, no pushing, no disorder or threat of riot. It is said that some of the group blocked part of the driveway leading to the jail entrance. The chief jailer to be sure testified that vehicles would not have been able to use the driveway. Never did the students locate themselves so as to cause interference with persons or vehicles going to or coming from the jail. Indeed, it is undisputed that the sheriff and deputy sheriff, in separate cars, were able to drive up the driveway to the parking places near the entrance and that no one obstructed their path. Further, it is undisputed that the entrance to the jail was not blocked. And wherever the students were requested to move they did so. If there was congestion, the solution was a further request to move to lawns or parking areas, not complete ejection and arrest. The claim is made that a tradesman waited inside the jail because some of the protestants were sitting around and leaning on his truck. The only evidence supporting such a conclusion is the testimony of a deputy sheriff that the tradesman "came to the door and then did not leave." His remaining is just as consistent with a desire to satisfy his curiosity as it is with a restraint. Finally the fact that some of the protestants may have felt their cause so just that they were willing to be arrested for making their protest outside the jail seems wholly irrelevant. A petition is nonetheless a petition, though its futility may make martyrdom attractive.

We do violence to the First Amendment when we permit this "petition for redress of grievances" to be turned into a trespass action. It does not help to analogize this problem to the problem of picketing. Picketing is a form of protest usually directed against private interests. I do not see how rules governing picketing in general are relevant to this express constitutional right to assemble and to petition for redress of grievances. In the first place the jailhouse grounds were not marked with "NO TRESPASSING!" signs, nor does respondent claim that the public was generally excluded from the grounds. Only the sheriff's fiat transformed lawful conduct into an unlawful trespass. To say that a private owner could have done the same if the rally had taken place on private property is to speak of a different case, as an assembly and a petition for redress of grievances run to government not to private proprietors.

The Court forgets that prior to this day our decisions have drastically limited the application of state statutes inhibiting the right to go peacefully on public property to exercise First Amendment rights. . . .

Such was the case of Edwards v South Carolina, supra, where aggrieved people "peaceably assembled at the site of the State government" to express their grievances to the citizens of the State as well as to the legislature. . . . Edwards was in the tradition of Cox v New Hampshire, . . . where the public streets were said to be "immemorially associated" with "the right of assembly and the opportunities for the communication of thought and the discussion of public questions.". . . When we allow Florida to construe her "malicious trespass" statute to bar a person from going on property knowing it is not his own and to apply that prohibition to public property we discard Cox and Edwards. Would the case be any different if, as is common, the demonstration took place outside a building which housed both the jail and the legislative body? I think not.

There may be some public places which are so clearly committed to other purposes that their use for the airing of grievances is anomalous. There may be some instances in which assemblies and petitions for redress of grievances are not consistent with other necessary purposes of public property. A noisy meeting may be out of keeping with the serenity of the statehouse or the quiet of the courthouse. No one, for example, would suggest that the Senate gallery is the proper place for a vociferous protest rally. And, in other cases it may be necessary to adjust the right to petition for redress of grievances to the other interests inhering in the uses to which the public property is normally put. . . . But this is quite different than saying that all public places are off-limits to people with grievances. . . . And it is farther yet from saying that the "custodian" of the public property in his discretion can decide when public places shall be used for the communication of ideas, especially the constitutional right to assemble and petition for redress of grievances. . . . For to place such discretion in any public official, be he the "custodian" of the public property, or the local police commissioner . . . is to place those who assert their First Amendment rights at his mercy. It gives him the awesome power to decide whose ideas may be expressed and who shall be denied a place to air their claims and petition their government. Such power is out of step with all our decisions prior to today where we have insisted that before a First Amendment right may be curtailed under the guise of a criminal law, any evil that may be collateral to the exercise of the right, must be isolated and defined in a "narrowly drawn" statute . . . lest the power to control excesses of conduct be used to suppress the constitutional right itself. . . .

That tragic consequence happens today when a trespass law is used to bludgeon those who peacefully exercise a First Amendment right to protest to government against one of the most grievous of all modern oppressions which some of our States are inflicting on our citizens. . . .

Today a trespass law is used to penalize people for exercising a constitutional right. Tomorrow a disorderly conduct statute, a breach of the peace statute, a vagrancy statute will be put to the same end. It is said that the sheriff did not make the arrests because of the views which petitioners espoused. That excuse is usually given, as we know from the many cases involving arrests of minority groups for breaches of the peace, unlawful assemblies, and parading without a permit. The charge against William Penn, who preached a nonconformist doctrine in a street in London, was that he caused "a great concourse and tumult of people" in contempt of the King and "to the great disturbance of the peace.". . . That was in 1670. In modern times also such arrests are usually sought to be justified by some legitimate function of government. Yet by allowing these orderly and civilized protests against injustice to be suppressed, we only increase the forces of frustration which the conditions of second-class citizenship are generating amongst us.

Appendix

1. THE SEDITION ACT OF JULY 14, 1798[1]

An Act in addition to the act, entitled "An act for the punishment of certain crimes against the United States."

SEC. 1. *Be it enacted . . .,* That if any persons shall unlawfully combine or conspire together, with intent to oppose any measure or measures of the government of the United States, which are or shall be directed by proper authority, or to impede the operation of any law of the United States, or to intimidate or prevent any person holding a place or office in or under the government of the United States, from undertaking, performing or executing his trust or duty; and if any person or persons, with intent as aforesaid, shall counsel, advise or attempt to procure any insurrection, riot, unlawful assembly, or combination, whether such conspiracy, threatening, counsel, advice, or attempt shall have the proposed effect or not, he or they shall be deemed guilty of a high misdemeanor, and on conviction, before any court of the United States having jurisdiction thereof, shall be punished by a fine not exceeding five thousand dollars, and by imprisonment during a term not less than six months nor exceeding five years; and further, at the discretion of the court may be holden to find sureties for his good behaviour in such sum, and for such time, as the said court may direct.

SEC. 2. That if any person shall write, print, utter, or publish, or shall cause or procure to be written, printed, uttered or published, or shall knowingly and willingly assist or aid in writing, printing, uttering or publishing any false, scandalous and malicious writing or writings against the government of the United States, or either house of the Congress of the United States, or the President of the United States, with intent to defame the said government, or either house of the said Congress, or the said President, or to bring them, or either of them, into contempt or disrepute; or to excite against them, or either or any of them, the hatred of the good people of the United States, or to stir up sedition within the United States, or to excite any unlawful combinations therein, for opposing or

[1] United States Statutes at Large, Vol. I, pp. 596–597.

resisting any law of the United States, or any act of the President of the United States, done in pursuance of any such law, or of the powers in him vested by the constitution of the United States, or to resist, oppose, or defeat any such law or act, or to aid, encourage or abet any hostile designs of any foreign nation against the United States, their people or government, then such person, being thereof convicted before any court of the United States having jurisdiction thereof, shall be punished by a fine not exceeding two thousand dollars, and by imprisonment not exceeding two years.

Sec. 3. That if any person shall be prosecuted under this act, for the writing or publishing any libel aforesaid, it shall be lawful for the defendant, upon the trial of the cause, to give in evidence in his defence, the truth of the matter contained in the publication charged as a libel. And the jury who shall try the cause, shall have a right to determine the law and the fact, under the direction of the court, as in other cases.

Sec. 4. That this act shall continue to be in force until March 3, 1801, and no longer. . . .

2. ESPIONAGE ACT OF JUNE 15, 1917, TITLE I, SECTIONS 3, 4 AND 5.[2]

Sec. 3. Whoever, when the United States is at war, shall willfully make or convey false reports or false statements with intent to interfere with the operation or success of the military or naval forces of the United States or to promote the success of its enemies and whoever, when the United States is at war, shall willfully cause or attempt to cause insubordination, disloyalty, mutiny, or refusal of duty, in the military or naval forces of the United States, or shall willfully obstruct the recruiting or enlistment service of the United States, to the injury of the service or of the United States, shall be punished by a fine of not more than $10,000 or imprisonment for not more than twenty years, or both.

Sec. 4. If two or more persons conspire to violate the provisions of sections two or three of this title, and one or more of such persons does any act to effect the object of the conspiracy, each of the parties to such conspiracy shall be punished as in said sections provided in the case of the doing of the act the accomplishment of which is the object of such conspiracy. Except as above provided conspiracies to commit offenses under this title shall be punished as provided by section thirty-seven of the Act to codify, re-

[2] United States Statutes at Large, Vol. XL, p. 219.

vise, and amend the penal laws of the United States, approved March fourth, nineteen hundred and nine.

SEC. 5. Whoever harbors or conceals any person who he knows, or has reasonable grounds to believe or suspect, has committed, or is about to commit, an offense under this title shall be punished by a fine of not more than $10,000 or by imprisonment for not more than two years, or both.

3. AMENDMENT OF MAY 16, 1918 TO SECTION 3 OF THE ESPIONAGE ACT OF 1917[3]

Whoever, when the United States is at war, shall willfully make or convey false reports or false statements with intent to interfere with the operation or success of the military or naval forces of the United States, or to promote the success of its enemies, or shall willfully make or convey false reports or false statements, or say or do anything except by way of bona fide and not disloyal advice to an investor or investors, with intent to obstruct the sale by the United States of bonds or other securities of the United States or the making of loans by or to the United States, and whoever, when the United States is at war, shall willfully cause or attempt to cause, or incite or attempt to incite, insubordination, disloyalty, mutiny, or refusal of duty, in the military or naval forces of the United States, or shall willfully obstruct or attempt to obstruct the recruiting or enlistment service of the United States, and whoever, when the United States is at war, shall willfully utter, print, write, or publish any disloyal, profane, scurrilous, or abusive language about the form of government of the United States, or the Constitution of the United States, or the military or naval forces of the United States, or the flag of the United States, or the uniform of the Army or Navy of the United States, or any language intended to bring the form of government of the United States, or the Constitution of the United States, or the military or naval forces of the United States, or the flag of the United States, or the uniform of the Army or Navy of the United States into contempt, scorn, contumely, or disrepute, or shall willfully utter, print, write, or publish any language intended to incite, provoke, or encourage resistance to the United States, or to promote the cause of its enemies, or shall willfully display the flag of any foreign enemy, or shall willfully by utterance, writing, printing, publication, or language spoken, urge, incite, or advocate any curtailment of pro-

[3] United States Statutes at Large, Vol. XL, p. 553.

duction in this country of any thing or things, product or products, necessary or essential to the prosecution of the war in which the United States may be engaged, with intent by such curtailment to cripple or hinder the United States in the prosecution of the war, and whoever shall willfully advocate, teach, defend, or suggest the doing of any of the acts or things in this section enumerated, and whoever shall by word or act support or favor the cause of any country with which the United States is at war or by word or act oppose the cause of the United States therein, shall be punished by a fine of not more than $10,000 or imprisonment for not more than twenty years, or both: *Provided,* That any employee or official of the United States Government who commits any disloyal act or utters any unpatriotic or disloyal language, or who, in an abusive and violent manner criticizes the Army or Navy or the flag of the United States shall be at once dismissed from the service. Any such employee shall be dismissed by the head of the department in which the employee may be engaged, and any such official shall be dismissed by the authority having power to appoint a successor to the dismissed official.

THE SMITH ACT OF 1940[4]

Whoever knowingly or willfully advocates, abets, advises, or teaches the duty, necessity, desirability, or propriety of overthrowing or destroying the government of the United States or the government of any State, Territory, District or Possession thereof, or the government of any political subdivision therein, by force or violence, or by the assassination of any officer of any such government; or

Whoever, with intent to cause the overthrow or destruction of any such government, prints, publishes, edits, issues, circulates, sells, distributes, or publicly displays any written or printed matter advocating, advising, or teaching the duty, necessity, desirability, or propriety of overthrowing or destroying any government in the United States by force or violence, or attempts to do so; or

Whoever organizes or helps or attempts to organize any society, group, or assembly of persons who teach, advocate, or encourage the overthrow or destruction of any such government by force or violence; or becomes or is a member of, or affiliates with, any such

---

[4] Originally passed as a section of Title I of the Alien Registration Act of 1940 (United States Statutes at Large, Vol. LIV, p. 670); now found in Title 18, United States Code, Section 2385.

society, group, or assembly of persons, knowing the purposes thereof—

Shall be fined not more than $10,000 or imprisoned not more than ten years, or both, and shall be ineligible for employment by the United States or any department or agency thereof, for the five years next following his conviction.

Table of Cases

Suggestions for Further Reading

For an historical perspective on the development of freedom of expression, reference should be made to the English origins of this important concept. One of the earliest statements in behalf of freedom of expression was made by John Milton, who used his great literary talents to fashion a plea for an uncensored press in the celebrated *Areopagitica*, 1644. This work may be found in *The Works of John Milton* (New York, 1931–38), compiled under the general editorship of Frank A. Patterson, specifically in volume 4, edited by William Haller. An early reference to freedom of speech as a civil liberty, distinct from freedom of the press and differentiated from a parliamentary right, was made in a series of essays (beginning in 1720) by John Trenchard and William Gordon, subsequently collected and published under the title, *Cato's Letters: Or, Essays on Liberty, Civil and Religious* (London 1755, 6th ed. 4 vols). Recent research has given a new status to these essays. Clinton Rossiter states that: "No one can spend any time in the newspapers, library inventories, and pamphlets of colonial America without realizing that *Cato's Letters* rather than Locke's *Civil Government* was the most popular, quotable, esteemed source of political ideas in the colonial period." Other works of note calling for toleration of political dissent and freedom of expression are *The Thoughts of A Tory Author* (London, 1712), generally ascribed to Joseph Addison, and *The Freedom of Speech and Writing upon Public Affairs, Considered with an Historical View* (London, 1766) by William Bollan. In the 19th Century, John Stuart Mill provides a rationale for freedom of expression in *On Liberty* (London, 1859). For a more systematic treatment of the development of freedom of expression in England, the student may wish to consult Thomas Erskine May's often cited and highly respected *Constitutional History of England* (New York, 1880).

In reference to our Colonial period, Clinton Rossiter's *Seedtime of the Republic* (New York, 1953) provides a general review of the men and ideas that shaped the American Revolution and the character of the national government. Two significant studies, specifically related to freedom of the press in the Colonial period, are by Livingstone R. Schuyler, *Liberty of the Press in the American Colonies Before the Revolutionary War* (New York, 1905), and, more recently, by Vincent Burnalolli, *The Trial of Peter Zenger* (New York, 1957). The latter volume contains notes on the famous trial which were made by James Alexander, Zenger's original lawyer, who was disbarred from the proceedings for accusing the trial judge of bias. Apparently James Alexander prepared the brief and planned the strategy of the trial and also secured the services of another lawyer, Andrew Hamilton, to whom history has accorded most of the credit for the victory. Another outstanding study on the status of free speech and press during the early and formative periods of American history is by Leonard W. Levy, *Legacy of Suppression* (Cambridge, 1960); from which the initial selection in the present volume is taken. For the origin of the first ten amendments and the politics involved in the adoption of them, see Robert Allen Rutland, *The Birth of the Bill of Rights, 1778–1791* (Chapel Hill, 1955), and for a short essay on congressional consideration of the first ten amendments see "Adoption of the Bill of Rights" in the appendix of *Fundamental Liberties of a Free People* (Ithaca, 1957) by Milton R. Konvitz. Undoubtedly, one of the most serious challenges to freedom of expression in the United States came with the passage of the Alien and Sedition Acts in 1798. John C. Miller in *Crisis in Freedom: The Alien and Sedition Laws* (Boston, 1951) and James Morton Smith's *Freedom's Fetters: The Alien and Sedition Laws and American Civil Liberties* (Ithaca, 1956) provide lively accounts of this turbulent period with its bitter political criticism and its prosecutions for seditious libel.

The literature on freedom of expression during the long stretch of American history from 1800 to the First World War is relatively sparse. One highly respected work related to that period is by Leon Whipple, *The Story of Civil Liberty in the United States* (New York, 1927). Whipple's study is particularly significant for it provides one of the rare discussions on the state of civil liberties in the two decades prior to 1860 and also records the restraints placed upon the press during the Civil War. Another work of distinction is a paper by Henry Schofield, "Freedom of the Press in the United States," Publication of the American Sociological Society, volume 9 (1914), published for the Sociological Society by the University of Chicago Press.

Since World War I there has been a notable increase in the volume of literature related to the First Amendment and to the problem of defining the limits of free expression. For insights into the strong nationalist sentiments that militated against political dissent during World War I, see John P. Roche's *Quest for the Dream* (New York, 1963); and for a vivid report on the 1920 campaign of the Department of Justice against the communist movement in the United States, see Robert K. Murray's *Red Scare* (Minneapolis, 1955). Harry N. Scheiber, in a monograph entitled, *The Wilson Administration and Civil Liberties,* 1917-1921 (Ithaca, 1960), provides a succinct and scholarly treatment of the Wilson Administration's policies toward civil liberty issues.

The clear-and-present-danger doctrine emerged from the cases prosecuted under the Espionage Acts of 1917 and 1918. Zechariah Chafee, Jr. has provided one of the most definitive and widely recognized studies of these cases and their impact on freedom of expression. Chafee, who was Langdell Professor of Law at Harvard University, first entered the field with *Freedom of Speech* (Cambridge, 1920). This book was designed to assist defense attorneys who were generally unfamiliar with free speech litigation. Later, as World War II progressed, Chafee's original work was revised, expanded, and published under the title, *Free Speech in the United States* (Cambridge, 1941). Chafee was sympathetic toward the clear-and-present-danger doctrine and was its chief exponent outside the Supreme Court. A more recent volume by Edward G. Hudon also treats the prosecutions under the Espionage Acts as a part of a general history of freedom of expression under the title of *Freedom of Speech and Press in America* (Washington, D. C., 1963). Also see Donald Johnson's *The Challenge to American Freedoms: World War I and The Rise of The American Civil Liberties Union* (Lexington, Kentucky, 1963) for the role played by the A.C.L.U. in protecting First Amendment freedoms.

One of the most distinguished and persistent critics of the clear-and-present-danger doctrine is Alexander Meiklejohn. His basic position, which tends toward the absolutist interpretation of the First Amendment, was set forth in *Free Speech and Its Relation to Self-Government* (New York, 1948). Meiklejohn has elaborated upon his interpretation of the First Amendment and the role of free expression in a democratic society in the following articles: "The First Amendment and Evils That Congress has a Right to Prevent," *Indiana Law Journal,* volume 26, (Summer, 1951) and "What Does the First Amendment Mean?" *University of Chicago*

Law Review, volume 20 (Spring, 1953). Another critic of the Holmes-
ian formula is Walter Berns, who argues in *Freedom, Virtue and
the First Amendment* (Baton Rouge, 1957) that the Constitution
should protect only that speech which is good, reasonable, and
civil in character. Since, in Berns' view, the clear-and-present-
danger doctrine does not draw the distinction between privileged
and illegal utterances on that basis, it stands condemned.

The doctrine of the preferred position was reflected most frequently in decisions of the Supreme Court during the decade from
1939 to 1949. The following are among the cases that reveal the
Court's preference for legal claims based on the First Amendment.
In *Thornhill v. Alabama,* 310 U.S. 88 (1940), picketing was held to
be a form of expression and thus protected by the First Amendment; in *Cantwell v. Connecticut,* 310 U.S. 269 (1940), solicitation
for religious purposes was sustained against the efforts of the state
to regulate it; in *West Virginia v. Barnette,* 319 U.S. 624 (1943),
the state was denied the authority to require the pledge of allegi-
ance and salute to the flag; and in *Terminello v. City of Chicago,*
337 U.S. 1 (1949), the right to speak was sustained even though
the speech had contributed to a public disturbance. Support for
the preferred-position approach to the First Amendment is given
by Charles L. Black, Jr. in *The People and the Court,* especially
chapter VII, (New York, 1960).

The prosecution of American communists under the Smith Act,
beginning in 1949 and extending into the mid-Fifties, precipitated
another debate on the limits of political discourse and evoked a
spate of writing on the subject. The fate of the clear-and-present-
danger doctrine is reflected in the title of an article by Edward S.
Corwin, "Bowing Out of Clear and Present Danger," *Notre Dame
Lawyer,* volume 27 (1951). Wallace Mendelson also contributed a
thoughtful article on the shifting meaning of the famous doctrine
in "Clear and Present Danger from Schenck to Dennis," *Columbia
Law Review,* volume 52 (1952). Thomas I. Cook supports the government's prosecution of the communists under the Smith Act in
Democratic Rights vs. Communist Activity (New York, 1954), while
Francis Biddle in *The Fear and Freedom* (New York, 1951) and
Sidney Hook in *Heresy, Yes—Conspiracy, No* (New York, 1953)
regard these prosecutions as misplaced attacks on freedom of
political expression. Robert G. McCloskey in "Free Speech, Sedition, and The Constitution," *The American Political Science Review*

(September, 1951), provides a general view of the Court's treatment of sedition and the First Amendment. For books that consider the relationship between the official policy toward domestic communists and freedom of expression, see Zechariah Chafee's *The Blessings of Liberty* (Philadelphia, 1956), Henry Steele Commager's *Freedom, Loyalty, Dissent* (New York, 1954), Walter Gellhorn's *Security, Loyalty, and Science* (Ithaca, 1950), Allen Maxwell's *The Present Danger* (Dallas, 1953), John Somerville's *The Communist Trials and the American Tradition* (New York, 1956), and Norman Thomas' *The Test of Freedom* (New York, 1954).

Frequently cases involving freedom of expression are enmeshed with the broader controversy on what role the Supreme Court should play in determining national policy, particularly when that policy impinges on rights protected by the Constitution. Judicial activists maintain that the Supreme Court should take a vigorous role in protecting claims based on the Bill of Rights, while the supporters of judicial restraint counsel that the Court should defer, if possible, to the policies established by legislative and executive authorities. These respective positions have been represented by Supreme Court Justice Black, who is oriented toward judicial activism, and by the late Justice Frankfurter, who was a vigorous proponent of judicial restraint. Wallace Mendelson, who supports the Frankfurter position, provides an analysis of the conflicting philosophies of these distinguished jurists in *Justices Black and Frankfurter* (Chicago, 1961). Judge Learned Hand also argues for judicial restraint in *The Bill of Rights* (Cambridge, 1958).

A judicial activist orientation is implicit in Justice Black's stand for the absolutist interpretation of the First Amendment. A convenient source for various opinions, speeches and occasional papers of Justice Black is a compilation edited by Irving Dillard entitled *Hugo LaFayette Black, One Man's Stand for Freedom* (New York, 1962). For a briefer review see Charles L. Black, "Mr. Justice Black, The Supreme Court, and The Bill of Rights," *Harpers Magazine* (February, 1961). In a recent work, Martin Shapiro focuses attention on the judicial activism v. judicial restraint controversy and its impact on questions involving freedom of expression. In *Freedom of Speech: The Supreme Court and Judicial Review* (Englewood Cliffs, New Jersey, 1966), Shapiro contends for the activist point of view. He does not go along, however, with Justice Black's absolutist view of the First Amendment. Instead, Shapiro argues that the Supreme Court should return to the clear-and-present-danger doctrine and the preferred position as guidelines for determining the scope of free expression.

A relatively new area of development for the First Amendment is in connection with the Negro civil rights movement. Protest marches and other types of demonstrations are non-verbal means of expressing grievances and the right to participate in such activities is based on the First Amendment. For an interesting review of these developments see Harry Kalven, *The Negro and the First Amendment* (Columbus, 1965).